Learning Englis

Grundgrammatik

Neubearbeitung

Lösungen zum Übungsbuch

Ernst Klett Verlag
Stuttgart Düsseldorf Leipzig

Learning English – Grundgrammatik
Ausgabe für Gymnasien – Neubearbeitung

Lösungen zum Übungsbuch (Klett-Nr. 511503)

9 783125 115057

1. Auflage 1 14 13 12 | 2017 2016 2015

Alle Drucke dieser Auflage können im Unterricht nebeneinander benutzt werden, sie sind untereinander unverändert.
Die letzte Zahl bezeichnet das Jahr dieses Druckes.

Internetadresse: http://www.klett-verlag.de

Redaktion: Inge Schäfer

Druck: Digitaldruck Tebben, Biessenhofen
Printed in Germany.
ISBN 3-12-511505-1

Contents

Chapter 1: Nouns

1 All in the family
1. cousin 2. sister 3. grandfather 4. aunts 5. son – daughter 6. nephew – niece 7 uncle 8. grandchild / granddaughter / grandson 9. father – uncle 10. husband / wife 11. his son

2 Nouns and pronouns
1. he 2. it / they 3. he / she 4. he / she 5. it / they 6. it / they / we 7. he / she 8. he / she 9. he / she 10. she 11. it / they 12. he / she / (it) 13. he / she 14. he / she 15. it / they 16. he / she 17. he / she 18. it / they 19. he / she 20. it / he

3 Using unusual nouns
1. glasses – them – they are 2. stairs – are – they are 3. furniture – it –it 4. police – them – they are 5. USA has 6. news – it 7. maths / mathematics is – it 8. trousers – they are – them – They look – them 9. scissors – don't cut. 10. hair looks – it 11. Fruit tastes – it's 12. Coal isn't used

4 Different expressions for different things
1. two pairs of trousers 2. a / one piece of cake 3. a / one pair of glasses 4. three pairs of scissors 5. a / one slice / piece of bread 6. a / one loaf of bread 7. two bottles of milk 8. three cups of tea 9. two pieces of luggage 10. a / one pair of shorts

5 What's that in English?
1. I can't decide between these two pairs of trousers. Can you give me some advice? 2. Why are the stairs to the first floor closed? I wanted to go to (the) ladies' clothes (department). – The police are here. They've closed the stairs. 3. Do we need anything else? – A loaf of bread, some milk and perhaps some cheese. 4. I've just been to / at the hairdresser's. Do you like my hair? – I'm sorry, but I liked it better when it was long. 5. We must / we'll have to look (it up) in the Internet. The information in this timetable isn't detailed enough. 6. Look what I've bought! Two pairs of jeans and a fantastic pair of shorts.

6 Regular and irregular plural forms
...s: beliefs, biros, chiefs, photos, proofs, roofs, videos
...es / ...oes: beaches, boxes, buses, churches, (fishes), buffaloes (or buffalo), heroes, potatoes, tomatoes
...ies: babies, cherries, countries, dictionaries, enemies
...ves: calves, knives, leaves, lives, thieves, wolves
singular = plural: aircraft, buffalo (or buffaloes), deer, fish, sheep
irregular forms: children, feet, mice, oxen, teeth, women

7 What is the difference?

1. The normal plural form is *fish. Fishes* refers to different kinds of fish. 2. You normally use the collective noun *fruit. Fruits* refers to different kinds of fruit, or to the results of something (e.g. "the fruits of our labours"). 3. *People* is a collective noun to refer to men, women and children. *Peoples* is the plural form of the countable noun *(a) people,* which refers to a nation or a tribe. 4. *Crisis* is the singular form *(a crisis), crises* is the plural form *(several crises).* 5. *passers-by, grown-ups*

Chapter 2 Personal and reflexive pronouns

1 Pronouns for persons

1. he – him 2. It – She – You – her 3. him 4. they 5. them 6. her – I – me 7. they

2 Trouble with the police

A motorist has been fined £20 for taking one hand off the steering wheel to eat a biscuit. Pat Storey, 33, says he / she was pulled up by police on the M3 for driving while not in proper control of his / her vehicle after they had seen him / her eating a chocolate biscuit. Pat had been taking his / her two children, James, 11, and Jacob, 2, to a birthday party when he / she was stopped near Winchester. He / She said that two officers told him / her that he / she had been driving at 68.7 mph in an area of roadworks limited to 50 mph but their equipment was not able to prove it. He / She said the police officers had told him / her that they had not stopped him / her for speeding but for driving while not in proper control of the vehicle. Pat said that he / she did a lot of driving in his / her job and that he / she hadn't taken the officers seriously. "I see everybody all the time talking on their mobile phones while they are steering and nobody stops them."

3 Say it with "they"

1. They've closed the motorway. 2. They're building a new bridge over the Thames. 3. They won't finish the new concert hall before Christmas. 4. When are they going to widen this road? 5. Why didn't they put up traffic lights here? 6. They often catch people for speeding on this stretch of road. 7. If they had spent less money on the new town hall, they could have built an open-air swimming pool.

4 *You* or *they*?

1. They – you – you 2. you 3. You – they 4. you 5. they 6. You – they

5 Do it yourself

2. must / will have to do it yourselves. 3. I cut it / did it myself. 4. he does it / everything himself 5. can / must / will have to do it / tidy it yourself 6. says anything / talks herself 7. we can do it ourselves 8. it was the King himself

6 Yesterday
1. feel – cut myself – behaved – happened – hurt yourself – acted – apologized
2. enjoy yourselves – wondered – help ourselves – worried

7 Rotkäppchen und Herr Wolf
Last night / Yesterday evening the musical *Little Red Riding Hood and the Wolf* had its premiere / first night on Broadway. The story is a very free version of the well-known fairy tale:
Little Red Riding Hood is on her way to her grandmother, whose house is in a dark forest. She hurries because it is already late and she is afraid of the dark. Suddenly she sees something moving / move behind the trees. It is a young man. He apologizes for frightening / having frightened her and says his name is Wolf. Little Red Riding Hood sees his big sad grey eyes and falls in love with him at once. She looks forward to seeing him again soon. But when they meet at the same place in the forest the next evening, something terrible has happened. The handsome young man / youth has changed a lot / (very much). He looks like a wolf.
Little Red Riding Hood runs to her grandmother's house. The latter / She is lying in bed and seems to be dead / as if she were dead. Little Red Riding Hood cannot imagine what (has) happened. She wonders desperately how she can help her grandmother. She feels unsure (of herself) and is unable to decide what to do. Suddenly the door opens and the young man enters / comes in. But he cannot remember her and ... Well, you will be surprised!

8 Mobile phones: Do you have one?
1. each other – each other – each other 2. themselves – themselves – themselves 3. each other – yourself – themselves

9 Different pronouns – different meanings
1. talk to each other 2. look after themselves 3. look after them 4. talk to themselves 5. look after each other 6. talk to them

Chapter 3: *S*-genitive, *of*-phrase and possessive words

1 By the seaside
1. the South West of England / England's South West 2. views of the coastline – the top of the cliffs 3. the residents' houses 4. Mike's grandparents – the middle of the town 5. his grandparents' house 6. his grandmother's two dogs – an hour's walk – the rest of the day 7. his grandfather's friends – the middle of the bay

2 Where exactly?
1. surgery 2. shop 3. office 4. cathedral 5. house 6. church 7. café 8. department store 9. restaurant 10. travel agency

3 Make up your mind, don't lose your head!
1. has injured her arm 2. fell off his bike – broke his leg(s) 3. lose their lives 4. took off our shoes 5. (have) changed our minds 6. shook her head 7. closed my eyes 8. put them in your pockets

4 Mein Opa
My grandfather is 78 and he's quite impossible / hopeless. Last year he fell off his motorbike and broke his arm. In the autumn, he climbed up a ladder to pick some apples. A strong wind blew into his face, and suddenly he lost his balance. He fell down and broke his leg. Last week he wanted to clean the seats of his car with petrol. While doing this he lit his pipe. My grandmother saved / rescued him from the burning garage. He owes his life to her. Yesterday he was standing there with his hands in his pockets and his pipe (a new one) in his mouth and said, "I have made up my mind / decided to climb Mount Everest." (He does not seem to know how many people have lost their lives there.)
My grandmother must love him with all her heart. He does not seem to get on **her** nerves. Only the neighbours' dog bares his / its teeth when he / it sees my grandfather.

5 My own TV
2. have their own swimming pool / a swimming pool of their own 3. has his own plane / a plane of his own 4. had their own TV / a TV of their own 5. her own horse / a horse of her own 6. has his own company / business / firm / a company / ... of his own 7. their own car / a car of their own

6 Yours or mine?
1. my – yours – mine – his 2. Their – theirs – theirs 3. our – ours 4. your – mine – yours – mine – hers 5. mine – yours

Chapter 4: Articles and demonstratives

1 Be careful with *the*
1. Do you like_Italian food? If so, you'll love the food at that new Italian restaurant. 2. I've just started a book about the life of Henry VIII. It gives a very interesting picture of_16th century life. 3. I usually take the bus to_school in the winter months, but I often go by_bike when it gets warmer. 4. Did you have_lunch on the plane? – Yes, but it wasn't as good as the lunch we had when we went to the Netherlands by_plane_last spring. 5. Can you tell me the way to_Buckingham Palace from here? – Go down_Queen Victoria Street until you get to the underground station. You can get to Westminster by_underground, and then walk to the palace through_St James's Park. 6. The Burtons can't come to_supper on_Friday after all –_poor Mrs Burton is ill.

2 Describing people
2. She's (working as) a shop assistant. 3. He wants to be an actor. 4. He's a Muslim. 5. She's a Scot / a Scotswoman. 6. She's an architect. 7. He's a socialist. 8. She's a capitalist. 9. His best friend is a Welshman.

3 How much? How fast? How often?
2. The wine is $14.90 a bottle. 3. The lions are fed once a day. 4. The speed limit on this road is 65 miles an hour. 5. She goes to the dentist's twice a year. 6. Single rooms are / cost $65 a night, double rooms $80 a night.

4 In London

a) The sight of the Houses of Parliament viewed from a bus crossing the River Thames at_Westminster Bridge makes_most British people feel patriotic and proud. Some people have the pleasure of seeing it five times a week, on their way to_work. But_people tend to forget that the Palace of Westminster is in_fact a place of work for over 1,700 people. Rather like a small village, the palace contains not only the chambers of the House of Commons and the House of Lords, as well as the offices of MPs and Lords, but also_bars,_restaurants, a gymnasium, a hair salon and a travel agency.

b) But the Tower of London is undoubtedly the capital's greatest historical sight. Today the Tower is famous as a tourist attraction, but at_different times in the past, it has been used as a fortress, a royal palace, a prison and a place of execution. Many of the people who came to the Tower as_prisoners were brought there by_boat. Two of the most famous prisoners were Anne Boleyn and Catherine Howard,_both of whom were wives of_King Henry VIII. Although they were_queens, they were sentenced to_death and lost their heads here. In the 16th century,_life was hard for_most people; even the life of a queen was not always safe for long!

c) In London,_public transport is excellent. Going by_underground is the fastest way to travel around. But if you take a / the bus, you can see some of the sights on the way. On the other hand, there is usually_heavy traffic on the streets of London. If you want to go from_Marble Arch to the British Museum, for_example, you'll be quicker on the underground than on a bus taking you along Oxford Street!

5 Saying it differently
2. Well, what a surprise! 3. He spent half the money he had. 4. Tim's got at least twice / double the number of CDs (that I have). 5. It was such a good party. 6. It's quite a good idea. 7. Let's play both the pieces. 8. Has Susan given all the cream to the cat? 9. Don't put the butter in too warm a place. 10. I usually only eat half the / a bar (of chocolate).

6 Was für eine Aussicht!
It was a beautiful morning when I arrived at the Empire State Building. The queue at the ticket offices already seemed to be half a mile long. But later in the day there are twice the number of visitors / there are twice as many visitors. The observatory is almost a quarter of a mile above Fifth Avenue. What a fantastic view! What a pity

that it had got cloudy / clouded over in the meantime. On cloudless / clear days you / one can see twice / double the distance / twice as far. Somebody said that it is / was foggy in New York half the time.
All the tourists were full of enthusiasm and took a lot of photos. But mobile phones were ringing all the time. I stayed up there for half an hour. When I went down again in the lift, I met Fritz from Neustadt. What a surprise!

7 That was stupid, wasn't it?
You know where we parked the car this morning? I can't remember the name of that street. Do you remember it? – Sorry, no. These street names here all sound the same, don't they? But didn't we leave it somewhere behind that park over there?
– Wait, let's look at this big street plan here. Now, this is the way we've come. And is that 22nd Street back there?
– Yes, it says S 22nd. – Hm, well, let's ask someone. Look at that patrol car parked across the street. Those officers are sure to help us find the car. I read somewhere that police officers these days are specially trained to deal with people like us. ...

Chapter 5: Expressions of quantity

1 Lost at sea in a dinghy
Imagine being in a rubber dinghy somewhere in the middle of the Atlantic Ocean for six days, without food or water. It may sound like something from an adventure story. But it really happened to Jenny Clark and her boyfriend Tim Davidson. The two young people had never experienced anything so terrible.
The horror trip began some hours after they had started on a sailing holiday. They were out in a yacht some miles off the coast of Spain when something exploded in the engine room. Then the boat caught fire. "It happened so quickly," says Jenny. "There wasn't anything anyone could do."
Soon they were both in the rubber dinghy. "We didn't have any time to put any food in the dinghy," explains Tim. "There wasn't even any chance to send an SOS." The yacht quickly went up in flames and sank.
The six days in the dinghy were a nightmare. They didn't have anything to eat and they didn't have any drinking water. "But we were lucky," says Jenny. "On some of the days it rained, so at least we could catch some of the rainwater."
Soon the weather got worse. "Someone once told me you get some pretty big waves in the Atlantic," says Tim. "I think some of the waves out there were 30 feet high or more. I've never seen anything like it anywhere."
Five ships passed before they were saved. "We waved and shouted, hoping desperately for someone to notice us," says Jenny. "But we couldn't get anyone's attention. In the end someone saw us. It was the sixth ship – and our sixth day in the dinghy."

2 Questions with a difference
1. some 2. some 3. any – some 4. something 5. Anything 6. anywhere 7. somewhere 8. anything – anyone / anybody 9. any 10. someone / somebody – something

3 What's that in English?
a) 1. I'm afraid / Unfortunately I have no time to tidy (up) my room now. 2. Are there no more stamps in the house? There are none in this drawer. 3. I opened the door, but there was no one / nobody there. 4. We can have the party at my house / place. My parents have (got) nothing against it. 5. I can't find my keys. They're nowhere here.
b) 1. ... I haven't got any time to tidy (up) my room now. 2. Aren't there any more stamps in the house? There aren't any in this drawer. 3. ... but there wasn't anyone / anybody there. 4. ... My parents haven't got anything against it. 5. I can't find my keys. They aren't anywhere here.

4 Sceptical questions
2. Well, how many mountains did you climb? 3. Well, how many grizzly bears did you see? 4. Well, how many hours did it take you? 5. Well, how much water did you drink? 6. Well, how many (thousands of) miles did you drive? 7. Well, how much gas did it use? 8. Well, how many casinos did you go to? 9. Well, how much money did you win? 10. Well, how many photographs did you take?

5 Little time and few chances
2. There wasn't much work to be done ... 3. ... She doesn't seem to have many friends. 4. There aren't many people nowadays ... 5. She is very busy all week and doesn't spend much time with her children. 6. I haven't got / don't have as / so much time today as I had yesterday. 7. Today not as / so many people smoke cigarettes as 20 years ago. 8. This Christmas I didn't spend as / so much as last year. I simply didn't buy as / so many presents, so I've got some money left. 9. If you have some / a bit of time, look at some of the museums in Washington. – I'm afraid I won't have enough time for sightseeing. 10. There wasn't much interest in the film, and not many people came to see it.

6 A little is better than hardly any
2. He spends a lot / lots (of money) on clothes every year. 3. There's plenty of / a lot of / lots of time. ... 4. A little / A bit of wine every day is very good for you. 5. There isn't any / There's no milk left, and hardly any yoghurt. 6. There are still a few / some pieces of cake left. There's still some / a bit of / plenty of / a lot of / lots of cake left. 7. Liza has lots of / a lot of CDs, but not many / hardly any / only a few are worth listening to. 8. There's some / a bit of butter in the fridge and some / a few eggs. 9. ... Now I haven't got much money left. / Now I have very little / hardly any money left. / Now I have still got some / a bit of money left.

7 Games
1. Every 2. everyone / everybody 3. everywhere 4. any 5. anyone / anybody 6. anything 7. everything 8. anywhere

8 Museum etiquette

... For the sake of our present and future visitors, however, we have rules that <u>everybody</u> must observe. We hope that these <u>few</u> rules do not cause <u>any</u> inconvenience.

- For the comfort of <u>all</u> visitors, and the protection of our collection, the Historical Center is a non-smoking facility.
- As almost <u>all</u> human body oils are acidic, <u>none</u> of the works of art should be touched. But there are <u>a few</u> objects in the Historical Center that are touchable and identified as such. <u>All</u> others should not be handled in <u>any</u> way.
- Strollers are provided for our small visitors, but they should be under the control of an adult <u>all the</u> time.
- <u>No</u> pets are allowed in the museum, so please leave them outside.
- Do not bring <u>any</u> weapons into the Historical Center.
- Leave <u>any</u> backpacks, motorcycle helmets, umbrellas and large containers in your car or check them into free lockers near the front door.
- <u>All</u> museum visitors are required to wear shirts and shoes; <u>no</u> bathing suits in the museum, please.

9 Parallel Lives

... This incredible tale is about THE PARALLEL LIVES of <u>two</u> people reunited through this newspaper.

We've had many happy endings before but none of them quite matches this one.

In the fifties <u>two</u> young people, Steve Smith and Gillian Potter, were still at school. <u>Both</u> went to Hargrove School in Bristol, and started going out together when they were 15 and 16. <u>Two</u> years later they got engaged. But then Steve went abroad and <u>the two</u> gradually drifted apart. <u>Neither</u> was very keen on writing, so in the end they lost contact and the engagement was broken off.

There have been extraordinary parallels in their lives. <u>Both</u> had happy but short marriages, which <u>both</u> came to an end when their partners were killed in traffic accidents in the very same year. Gillian and Steve <u>both</u> have one son. <u>Both</u> young men are keen on rugby and they <u>both</u> play for their county.

Gillian and Steve have been living on their own for exactly fifteen years now. <u>Neither</u> has ever thought of getting married again. They <u>both</u> used to work in the banking business and retired last year.

Our paper traced Gillian, who lives in North London, through her sister. Then Steve, who later returned to Bristol, went to visit his old sweetheart – after 44 years. When we talked to Gillian she said, "We were <u>both</u> rather lonely people. Now there is a lovely second chance for <u>the two / both</u> of us." She doesn't know yet whether they will live together in Bristol or in London. "<u>Either</u> place will be fine." she smiled.

10 Stay at the Belmont

- ➩ The Belmont in Chicago is the ideal hotel for all travellers and business people.
- ➩ There is a lot to see in Chicago, and many of the most famous sights can be reached on foot or by taxi. There is also a shuttle bus to the city centre for our guests: departure every 20 minutes from the main entrance (Michigan Avenue).
- ➩ LaSalle Street, the financial centre of the city, is only a few blocks (of houses)

away, and it is only a few minutes through Grant Park to the shore of Lake Michigan.

⇨ But actually nobody has to / needs to leave the hotel. The five shops on the ground floor sell all kinds of / every kind of gifts and luxury goods / gifts and luxury goods of all kinds / every kind.

⇨ The two restaurants on the 10th floor are famous for their excellent food. Both are run by well-known French chefs.

⇨ All our rooms have a fantastic view of the lake, and each (one) / every one is luxuriously furnished. Many even have two separate bathrooms.

⇨ Our two huge conference rooms are at your disposal as well as our many smaller rooms. So we are able / This enables us to organize any event, from small business meetings to giant exhibitions.

11 A puzzle

a) **Across:** 4. every 6. nothing 7. few 10. all 11. both 12. many 13. everywhere 15. something 17. neither 19. everyone 20 anywhere
Down: 1. lot 2. plenty 3. any 5. either 6. nowhere 8. none 9. someone 10. anything 12. much 14. little 16. no 18. each

b) **Across:** 4. (Es gibt) keine Regel ohne Ausnahme. 6. Es gibt nichts Neues unter der Sonne. 7. Viele sind berufen, aber wenige sind auserwählt. 10. Nachts sind alle Katzen grau. 11. Man kann nicht von allem nur das Beste haben wollen. (Man kann nicht das Beste von beiden Welten haben). 12. Zu viele Köche verderben / versalzen den Brei. 13. Alles hat seinen Preis. (Es gibt nichts umsonst.) 19. Allen Leuten recht getan ist eine Kunst, die keiner kann. (Man kann es nicht jedem recht machen.) **Down:** 3. Irgendeine Entschuldigung ist besser als gar keine. 8. Niemand ist blinder als der, der nicht sehen will. 10. Was immer schief gehen kann, geht auch schief. 12. Allzu viel ist ungesund. (Man kann zu viel des Guten haben.) 13. Mäßigkeit erhält den Leib. / Alles mit Maß. (Ein bisschen von dem, worauf du Lust hast, tut dir gut.) 16. Kein Rauch ohne Feuer.

Chapter 6: Prepositions in expressions of time and place

1 Special days

1. Small children are always very excited at Christmas time. In Britain, they don't get their presents on Christmas Eve, but on Christmas Day. When they go to bed on the evening of Christmas Eve, a lot of children try to stay awake. They know that Santa Claus always comes down the chimney late at night with their presents, but when? Will he come at midnight this year? Or at one o'clock in the morning? Then, on the morning of December 25th, when they wake up and find their presents at the foot of the bed, they realize they must have fallen asleep in the night, *before* he came, just like the year before!
2. Easter is in March this year. On Good Friday we sometimes go to church. There is a special service that starts at noon and finishes at 3 o'clock in the afternoon.
3. My birthday is in July. It's nice to have it in the summer, because I usually have a party on my birthday, and we sometimes have a barbecue. It stays light nice and long in the evenings at that time of the year.

2 What's that in English?

1. My train leaves at half past nine on Monday. 2. I will only be away for three days. 3. Hurry up, please. We wanted to leave by quarter to eight (at the latest). 4. I haven't been to the cinema for weeks. 5. How long have you been living here? – Since September. We moved exactly eight weeks ago. 6. Would you like the appointment in the morning, or would you prefer to come between three and four in the afternoon? 7. I'd like to go skiing again next winter. 8. Are you staying / going to stay until New Year's Day / New Year? – Yes, we're staying from Thursday to Tuesday. We aren't leaving until 2nd January.

3 On the train

Jack had got on / into / in the train at Reading. At first he had been on his own, but at the next stop some people had come into his compartment, an elderly couple. They had put their luggage on the rack above Jack's head: two large suitcases and a birdcage, balanced on the smaller of the cases. It looked dangerous. If the train braked suddenly, it might fall down and crash on(to) Jack's head. The man was sitting at / near / by the window, his wife beside / next to him. They had a large, angry-looking dog with them It was lying on the floor between the man's legs, its open mouth uncomfortably near / close to Jack's ankles.
There was a No Smoking sign on the opposite wall. The man took a large cigar out of / from a leather case, lit it and blew the smoke straight into Jack's face. Jack got up, almost fell over / on(to) the dog, and then stepped on(to) its tail. He just managed to get out of the compartment, the dog furiously barking at / behind the door. The train was going up a hill now, moving slowly along its tracks. It was peaceful in the next compartment. Jack looked out of the window. It was a wonderful morning, not a single cloud in the sky. The train was going past a small farm. He noticed some cows in a field and an old tractor parked by / near a fence. Some large black birds were sitting on the fence. A farmer was walking across / through / over the

field towards / to the cows. A small dog ran in front of / before him, sometimes looking back at its slow master. Jack closed his eyes and started to dream.
The farmer's little dog jumped over the fence and started to run after the train. And it was getting bigger and bigger. It caught up with the train and ran beside / towards Jack's carriage now. And then it jumped and crashed through the window, pushed Jack against the wall, its great white teeth at / near his throat.
He screamed. There was a strange man in front of / before him. "Tickets please," said the ticket collector. "Everything OK, sir?"

4 *By* or *with*? *After* or *behind*?
1. The policeman ran after the burglar, but lost sight of him because the burglar had hidden behind a tree. 2. Robin Hood always shared out the stolen money among the poor. 3. At that time there were big / great social differences between the Norman rulers and the Anglo-Saxons. 4. Eric lived with his grandparents in Australia for many years. And he often spent his summer holidays at his aunt's in Sydney. 5. The parents told me to / said I should look after the baby until 10 o'clock, but they didn't come home until / till 12 o'clock. 6. I won't stay in (the) town long. I'll be back (here) by half past three.

Chapter 7: Adjectives

1 Asleep or sleeping?
1. sleeping 2. frightened 3. asleep 4. lone 5. alive 6. afraid 7. Living 8. alone

2 It didn't taste too bad!
The idea of going to this old fish and chip shop didn't sound / seem very exciting. But Marion had asked me to come and she always gets / feels / seems upset when people don't want to do what she suggests. So I went, although I didn't feel hungry at all.
It was fairly late, and it was already getting / growing dark when we got near the shop. We could soon tell we were getting near the shop because it smelt / smelled so strong. But the food was / seemed / tasted alright, and the fish actually tasted delicious. (The chips were / tasted a little oily, though.) When I had eaten about half of it, I started to feel funny. Marion said, "Your face has gone green, I hope you won't be / get sick." "Oh, be quiet, Marion," I said and ran to the door.

3 Everything all right?
Everything seemed so nice and harmonious, when Sarah suddenly said, "This soup smells funny / strange, doesn't it?" "I don't know. I can't smell very well with my cold. Does it taste funny / strange, too / as well?" She took her spoon and tasted the soup slowly and carefully. "It tastes awful / terrible / horrible. Let's call the waitress." The waitress was very slow, and I noticed Sarah getting angry / saw that Sarah was getting angry. "Keep calm / cool," I said. The waitress came to our table. She looked serious / grave and looked at us critically, but seemed to feel unsure (of herself) / insecure. "Is everything all right / alright / OK?" she asked. Her voice did not sound very friendly.

4 The comparison of adjectives

Basic form	Comparative form	Superlative form
astonishing	more astonishing	most astonishing
bad	worse	worst
big	bigger	biggest
busy	busier	busiest
clever	cleverer	cleverest
far	further / farther	furthest / farthest
fit	fitter	fittest
good	better	best
late	later	latest
many	more	most
much	more	most
narrow	narrower	narrowest
quiet	quieter	quietest
simple	simpler	simplest

5 The greatest sporting show on Earth

a) The following events are to be compared in pictures 2 to 8:
2. basketball – hockey 3. swimming – diving 4. the marathon – the 100 metres 5. wrestling – boxing 6. football – tennis 7. the high jump – the long jump 8. rowing – sailing

c) 1. In a normal bicycle race, the fastest cyclist is the winner. In a slow-bicycle race the slowest cyclist is the winner. 2. The winner has not arrived yet, because he is slower than the winners of the silver and bronze medals.

6 What's that in English?

1. The hotter the day (is / gets / becomes), the more strenuous / tiring the marathon (is / gets / becomes). 2. During the last few years, the Games have become more and more spectacular and the number of competitors higher and higher / greater and greater / larger and larger. 3. Although the 100 meters is shorter than all the other races, the preparations and the training are just as important as with the longer distances. 4. Many / A lot of people find synchronized swimming the least interesting of all the Olympic events. 5. The most important thing / What is most important in the Olympic Games is not winning but taking part.

7 Yellowstone National Park

- Yellowstone has been a national park since 1872. In fact it is the oldest in the USA.
- It has the highest / greatest concentration of wildlife in the lower mainland USA (with buffalo and grizzly bears being the most impressive / spectacular / exciting / famous / popular but also the most dangerous among them).
- While Yellowstone has become the most popular / famous of America's national parks, its popularity has at the same time become the greatest threat to its environment.
- Yellowstone's highest mountain is Mount Washburn (10,243 feet), and the

Grand Canyon of the Yellowstone is one of the most famous / impressive / spectacular canyons in the world.

- ✿ Yellowstone has the world's largest / most famous / impressive / spectacular active geyser field, and its most famous / impressive / popular active geyser is Old Faithful.
- ✿ One of the Yellowstone geysers is called Steamboat. Steamboat's eruptions are the most forceful / highest in the world, with steam and water shooting up to over 300 feet.
- ✿ But while Old Faithful's eruptions are (the) most frequent (an eruption occurs about every 80 minutes), Steamboat erupts very irregularly – only twice in the last ten years.

8 This one and that one

2. a black one and a grey one. 3. an expensive one and a cheap one / a more expensive one and a cheaper one. 4. old ones and a new / modern one. 5. the smaller ones. 6. the long(er) one or the short(er) one?

9 Famous sayings

a) 1. a rich man 2. the rich – the poor 3. the hungry – the rich 4. the rich man – the poor man 5. a rich man 6. the blind – the blind 7. the blind – the one-eyed man 8. A blind wife – a deaf husband 9. the young – the old

b) 4. Der Reiche hat sein Eis im Sommer, und der Arme bekommt es im Winter. 5. Eher geht ein Kamel durch ein Nadelöhr, als ein Reicher in den Himmel. 7. Im Land der Blinden ist der Einäugige König. 8. Eine blinde Ehefrau und ein tauber Ehemann sind immer ein glückliches Paar.

10 Quick translation

1. young people 2. the little one / boy 3. the dead woman 4. a blind man 5. many / a lot of disabled / handicapped people 6. two blacks 7. the unemployed 8. the living and the dead (NB: The biblical equivalent is "the quick and the dead") 9. a group of homeless people 10. the bad thing about it 11. the Conservatives 12. a sick man / person

11 Countries, people and languages

2. a Belgian – The Belgians speak Flemish and French.
3. a Briton – The British speak English, (Welsh and Gaelic).
4. Canada – The Canadians speak English and French.
5. a Chinese – The Chinese speak Chinese / (Cantonese, Mandarin and Pekingese).
6. Denmark – The Danes / The Danish speak Danish.
7. an Englishman / an Englishwoman. – The English speak English.
8. a Frenchman / a Frenchwoman. – The French speak French.
9. Germany – The Germans speak German.
10. an Irishman / an Irishwoman – The Irish speak English and Gaelic / Irish.
11. Italy – The Italians speak Italian.
12. a Dutchman / a Dutchwoman – The Dutch speak Dutch.
13. Poland – The Poles / The Polish speak Polish.

14. a Portuguese – The Portuguese speak Portuguese.
15. Turkey – The Turks / The Turkish speak Turkish.
16. an American / a US American – The Americans speak English. (Many also speak Spanish.)
17. Wales – The Welsh speak English and Welsh.

Chapter 8: Adverbs and adverbial phrases

1 Adjective or adverb?

a) **How music can drive motorists crazy**

Road rage is an enormous problem in Britain. It is well known that our drivers are among the most aggressive in Europe. Many like to drive fast, and at the same time they like to listen to deafeningly loud music. Experts warn that this is actually no coincidence. Playing powerful music in the car can lead people to drive more dangerously than they otherwise would. In traffic jams, rock music with a heavy bass makes us want to move forward fast, but since this is not possible, we become angry and frustrated. Being surrounded by rock or dance music in a place where your movements are severely restricted, as they are in a car, unfortunately tends to block out the part of the brain that normally deals with logical reasoning.

Radio disc jockeys are conscious of the psychological effect of music on drivers in heavy traffic. But they usually argue that slow or sad music only makes people drive too slowly!

In the Netherlands, where road rage is also something that confronts motorists daily, the whole problem is taken very seriously. There is a new CD of truly calming music, whose title can be translated as "Easy Driver".

b) There are basically two types of "road rage drivers". The first are the people who usually / normally behave aggressively and impatiently in everyday situations anyway. So it doesn't take long to make them angry on the road. The second are those who are normally / usually calm and peaceful but unfortunately react very differently / aggressively / angrily / impatiently on the road.

If another driver reacts aggressively / angrily / impatiently to something you have done, you are advised not to look at the other driver directly, and if possible to drive away immediately / quickly. If you are trapped, you should quickly / immediately lock your doors. Recognizing a danger as early / quickly as possible is essential.

2 Calvin at school

1. hard – lately 2. pretty – hardly 3. late – just 4. fairly / pretty – fair – justly 5. prettily

3 Spurs v United

Spurs have trained very hard for weeks. But nevertheless they will hardly have a chance against United on Saturday. They have a number of fairly / pretty / rather /

quite good players and are highly motivated, but most United stars are world-class. And they have just won the final of the Champions League. But Spurs have improved lately, too, and especially the second half of the last away match was really pretty / fairly / rather / quite impressive. Too bad that Tony Richards will not be able to play. A player who / that (has) played extremely fair (for) the whole (of the) season suddenly saw red during the last home match and was justly sent off the field. He had tried to stop Liverpool's John Adams, but unfairly and much / far too late. This unfair tackling was justly penalized / punished by a suspension of three weeks / a three-week suspension.

4 Workers of the world – in London

1. I came to London 18 months ago. Luckily I quickly adapted to life in London / I adapted to life in London quickly. My English boyfriend has always lived here in London.
2. Unfortunately life here is very hard for me / life is very hard for me here. I started a course at a drama school in September / In September I started a course at a drama school. I have to go to school in the morning every day / Every day I have to go to school in the morning / In the morning I have to go to school every day. Then I always work here in the afternoon / In the afternoon I always work here then / Then in the afternoon I always work here.
3. I settled down here pretty quickly. I have already spent two months with this company / I have spent two months with this company already. I will probably return to Korea again next February / Next February I will probably return to Korea again. Maybe I will come back to Britain again later.
4. People from different countries are fully accepted here / Here people from different countries are fully accepted. Actually, only nine of our 46 employees are British / Of our 46 employees only nine are actually British. / British, actually.

5 Punch and Judy shows

1. Summer time is Punch and Judy time at many seaside towns in Britain every year. / At many seaside towns in Britain, summer time is Punch and Judy time every year. / In Britain, summer time is Punch and Judy time at many seaside towns every year. / Every year summer time is Punch and Judy time at many seaside towns in Britain. 2. The Codman family first started their own family tradition of Punch and Judy shows in Llandudno, Wales, in 1860. / In 1860, the Codman family first started their own family tradition of Punch and Judy shows in Llandudno, Wales. 3. Amazingly, Jackie Codman and her husband Morris still carry it on in the same place today. 4. They still use the puppets originally made by Jackie's great-grandfather, Richard Codman, all those years ago. 5. Jackie often spends the winter months busily making new dresses for the puppets and carefully repainting their faces / Jacky spends the winter months busily ... and often carefully .... 6. They perform four 45-minute shows daily in a space not much bigger than a telephone box. / Daily they perform ... / They daily perform ... 7. Naturally they are very proud of the family tradition. 8. Londoners were however actually the first ever to see / to ever see a Punch puppet show in Britain in 1622. / However, Londoners were actually the first ... / Londoners, however, were actually the first ... / Londoners were actually the first, however, to ... 9. Punch's birthday is still cele-

brated in the grounds of St Paul's Church, Covent Garden, on March 14th every year.

6 Links between violent games and aggressive behaviour?

Playing violent video games is **apparently** more harmful / **Apparently** playing video games is more harmful than watching violence on TV. Interactive computer games require players to identify with the characters carrying out the violence – **so** they **obviously** increase aggressive thoughts and behaviour. **Moreover,** a recent scientific study found that students who played the most computer games did worst at college. **Of course,** not every child that plays computer games becomes aggressive. But **not surprisingly** young men who are habitually aggressive are more vulnerable to the effects of violent games.

In fact, even a short exposure to video games can increase aggressive behaviour. **In the short run,** playing a violent video game appears to encourage violent thoughts. There aren't any reliable statistics about long term effects, **though. Yet** this medium is **probably** more dangerous than violent television and movies.

Not surprisingly the producers of these games say that there is **clearly** no link between violent games and aggressive behaviour. **In fact** they claim that most video games contain little or no violence. And **in the end** it is the parents' job to make sure that their kids play the right games. **Nevertheless** there are many critics that **actually** demand / **Nevertheless** there are **actually** many critics that demand / There are **nevertheless** many critics that **actually** demand that the industry should stop producing these games altogether. **After all,** their children might be affected too, **of course**.

7 A few days in Ireland

1. We try to go to England at least once a year. But last year / Last year, however, we didn't go to England, but to Wales / we weren't in England, but in Wales. From there we went to Ireland by ferry for a few days. We arrived in Dublin at about four o'clock in the afternoon. 2. We wanted to stay in the Republic of Ireland for the first two days and then go on to Northern Ireland. You can't drive fast on the narrow roads in Ireland. But the landscape / scenery / countryside is so incredibly / unbelievably beautiful, that you actually never want to drive fast. 3. Surprisingly, the weather in Ireland was lovely / wonderful the whole (of the) time / all the time. 4. On the second evening, we were in a small place / town / village on the border between the Republic and Northern Ireland. When we went up to our rooms on the second floor, the landlord came out of / from the pub on the ground floor and asked us if we would like to come down for a glass of Guinness. 5. On that evening, an Irish band was playing in the pub. They were playing / played extremely well, and we easily got into conversation with the other guests / customers in the pub. That was surely / certainly one of the best experiences I have ever had on holiday. 6. Unfortunately we had to get up at seven o'clock the next morning and go / travel on.

Chapter 9: The tenses of the verb

1 The encounter
... He usually leaves at this time of day. He shuts the door behind him, runs down the stairs from the third floor and goes out into the street. Outside it is raining. Normally Johnny walks the few blocks to his favourite bar. But the rain is getting heavier now. So he decides to take a cab. Traffic is moving very slowly. But at last a cab stops. He gets in and tells the driver where to go. When they get to the bar, Johnny sees a man near the entrance. He looks familiar, although he is standing with his back to Johnny. For a moment Johnny does not know who he is. Then he remembers. "Razor Charlie! How on earth did he get out of jail?" Johnny wonders. "Is he waiting for me?" Suddenly the man turns round. There is something in his hand, it is glittering in the lights of the cars that are driving past.

2 Which is correct?
1. do you do – read – am reading 2. am not enjoying – think – are being 3. is getting – gets – doesn't 4. am beginning – is always taking – ever want – always ask

3 Her holiday job
"What are you doing all the time, Christine? I never see you in (the) town." "I've got this holiday job. I'm working at the moment, and I want to make / earn some money. I'm taking driving lessons. And that costs a lot of money. But some people just have rich parents." "Very funny. By the way, I'm working, too. I'm doing this intensive course in English, four hours a day, pretty hard / tough. But I think / believe (that) I'm beginning to get better / I'm gradually getting / I'm improving slowly. You know what marks I have in English. And you, what exactly are **you** doing? Where are you working?" "I'm working at / in the pub near / at the station. I'm enjoying it very much – at least at the moment. The pub doesn't open until midday / noon, so (that) I don't have to / needn't get up so early. But it doesn't close until midnight. I always meet a lot of interesting people. Sometimes a few / some Americans come to / into the pub, too. But of course I don't learn as much English as you (do) in your intensive course. – Oh, it's getting late, I'll have to / I must go now. Bye, Markus."

4 At Heathrow Airport
2. They have been waiting for two and a half hours. 3. It has broken down. 4. He has been working for seven hours. 5. She hasn't ordered (anything) yet. 6. They have been there for several hours. 7. She has forgotten her passport. 8. They have been sitting on the plane for over an hour.

5 *Since* or *for*?
1. I've been looking forward to this film for ages! 2. It has only been on since Wednesday. 3. I haven't been to the cinema for weeks. 4. I haven't seen a really good film since my birthday. 5. Sarah has been working for the BBC in London for two years. 6. John's new girlfriend is an actress. They have known each other for a few months. 7. Let's go outside a bit. We've been sitting in front of the TV for hours!

6 Scared to death

1. "It happened a few years ago. My brother and I were playing in the park. We had his go-kart with us, and I persuaded him to let me ride it down the steep hill there. I got on and rode off, but after a few moments I realized that the go-kart was getting faster and faster – and I didn't know how to stop it! There was a busy main road at the bottom of the hill, and the traffic on it was moving fast. When I saw it, I thought: 'This is it, I'm going to die!' At the last moment, as the go-kart was racing through the big park gates, a miracle happened. The traffic lights changed, and all the cars stopped, and the go-kart just sailed through the middle."
2. "I was looking after my two younger sisters one day when our mum was out. We were eating nuts when suddenly Jodie, my youngest sister, swallowed a whole nut and started to choke . It was awful. She was getting / got blue in the face, and my other sister was shouting / shouted at me to do something. I knew there was no time to call an ambulance. So I picked Jodie up by her ankle and held her upside down. Then, while I was holding her like that, I hit her on the back, really hard, until the nut came shooting out. When Mum got home, the three of us were sitting there in floods of tears. I was crying from shock, and my sisters because I had hit Jodie so hard on the back!"

7 Travelling

1. have been sitting 2. had 3. Have – come – haven't 4. Did – have – were – have never known – were staying – started 5. haven't seen 6. Has – rung up – went 7. was waiting – got 8. Have – written – sent 9. has been living / has lived – haven't visited 10. Did – visit – went – didn't have

8 Australia – nation of colonies

European settlement of Australia began in 1788, when a British penal colony was founded on the east coast, at a place which since then has developed into the great city of Sydney. All in all, six colonies were eventually established in Australia, but it was not until 1901 that they all joined together as a federation. Before that year, each area had its own system of taxes and laws; there were even different postage stamps for the different colonies!

Since January 1st 1901, Australia has been one nation. But even today, differences between the individual states have not yet disappeared entirely. Although the borders between the states have all been abolished, the fact that each state issues its own driving licence has not changed so far. Trains have only been able to travel from one state to another since the 1980s; before that this was not possible because the width of the tracks varied from state to state.

When the new nation was declared in 1901, it needed a capital. Rivalry between the two biggest cities in New South Wales and Victoria, Sydney and Melbourne, was so great that it was eventually agreed to build a new city as a capital somewhere in the bush. But although Canberra has since then become one of the nation's largest cities, it has never been able to match the other Australian cities for flair. It has remained a quiet city of parks, trees, plazas – and government buildings.

9 Wyatt Earp

2. After young Wyatt Earp had travelled all over the country, he started to work on the construction of the Union Pacific Railway. 3. After he had served as a deputy and marshal for several towns in Illinois, his wanderings finally led him to Tombstone. 4. Although Wild Bill Hickock had taught him how to shoot in Kansas City, Wyatt preferred to settle fights without the aid of firearms. 5. Soon after Wyatt had arrived in Tombstone in the fall of 1879, he was appointed deputy sheriff of this wild and dangerous place. / In the fall of 1879, soon after he had arrived in Tombstone, Wyatt was appointed deputy sheriff ... 6. Before Wyatt Earp succeeded in reducing crime in Tombstone, the Clanton Gang had "run" the town. 7. "Old Man" Clanton decided to kill the sheriff, because Wyatt Earp's activities had begun to affect their "business interests". 8. Although Wyatt Earp had been warned to keep away from the Clantons and their followers, he and his friend Doc Holliday went to meet them at the OK Corral. 9. When the dust had settled after a 30-second shootout, two of the Clantons were dead, and one was badly wounded. 10. When the Clantons had taken their revenge and (had) shot two of Wyatt's brothers, Wyatt got tired of fighting and left Tombstone.

10 Why Charles I lost his head

When Elizabeth I died in 1603, she had been on the throne for 45 years. As she had (had) no children, the crown (was) passed to her cousin, James Stuart. James had been King of Scotland since he was a baby. He now became the first person to rule both countries. After his death in 1625, his son Charles I succeeded him.

For centuries Parliament and the Monarch had been arguing about which of the two was more powerful. Charles believed in the "Divine Right of Kings". He had been taught by his father that kings were appointed by God and that the people had to obey the king. After he had ruled / had been ruling the country without Parliament for 11 years, Charles had to call Parliament because he needed money for his family and for war with Scotland. It had always been Parliament's right to raise taxes. After Charles had listened / had been listening to the complaints of the MPs for days, he lost patience and sent them away. But soon after, he had to call them again because his army had been beaten by the Scots and Charles had promised to pay money to the victorious army.

When Parliament demanded that Charles should share command of a new army with the MPs, he believed they wanted to take all his power. He stormed into Parliament with his soldiers, wanting to arrest five leading MPs. But they had been warned beforehand and (had) escaped. When Parliament now started to pass laws that the King had not agreed to, he raised an army.

Parliament raised an army, too. War began / had begun. The Royalists and the Parliamentarians had been fighting for six years, when finally the King was captured in 1648. After he had been tried in court and (had been) found guilty, he was executed in 1649. The trial and execution of the King by his own subjects was something that had never happened in England before. But Parliament had won the struggle.

11 What is going to happen?

2. Germany is / are going to win. (c) 3. The ship / The Titanic is going to sink. (c)

4. He is going to steal the man's purse / wallet. (p) 5. He is going to have a frightful crash. (c) 6. He is going to cut off a / the branch. (p) 7. She is going to fall into the (man)hole. (c) 8. He is going to be late (for school). (c) 9. He is going to play (the trumpet). (p) 10. It is going to rain. (c)

12 Spontaneous decisions
2. I'll have tea. 3. I'll show you how to do it. 4. I'll lend you mine / one (of mine). 5. I'll do / help you with the washing-up. 6. I'll send you a postcard. 7. I'll get some. 8. I won't tell anyone.

13 Plans and their results
2. I'm going to take the early train. Then I'll have lots of time in town. 3. I'm going to buy this one. It'll go with my new skirt. 4. I'm going to add (some) more wine. Then it will taste great. 5. I'm going to practise hard. Then I'll get really good. 6. I'm going to learn my / the words. Then I'll do well in the test.

14 Ranger programs
On Tuesday morning I'll be explaining about fire managing techniques (together with a firefighter).
On Wednesday afternoon I'll be taking tourists for a walk on the rim of the Grand Canyon.
On Thursday evening / night I'll be telling stories and singing songs by the / a campfire.
On Friday evening / night I'll be showing tourists / we'll be looking at the Milky Way and other wonders of the night sky.
On Saturday I'll be showing tourists / we'll be looking at / watching the changing colors of the (Grand Canyon at) sunset.

15 Arrangements and predictions
1. I'm going to America. – I'm staying with my grandfather in Chicago. – He'll be 75 next month. 2. Yes, it will be sunny in the morning and wet later. 3. My train leaves at 9.20. 4. The play starts at 8 p.m. – We're / I'm / Someone is / collecting her at half past seven. – We're going to McDonalds.

16 Invading England
"My friends, we have been waiting a long time now, and I can understand that you're getting impatient. But I'm sure that this long wait will end very soon. As soon as the wind changes, we will sail to England. And don't worry about the battle. We are going to win the day. I'm sure that our superbly trained war-horses will frighten the English foot-soldiers away. And, very probably, our arrows will rain death on them. We will not stop fighting until we have won. And I hope, friends, that God will be with us.
As soon as we have won the battle, we will make for London. Believe me, friends, in three weeks' time the Londoners will have welcomed us with open arms and we will be marching into that great city.
I expect there will be little resistance. But if there is, we will build strong castles. You, my knights, are going to be the masters of those castles, and the masters of

England. And when I have been crowned in Westminster Abbey, I will be King of England!!! When I am King, all of you will be rewarded richly. And if God is with us, we will build great cathedrals to thank Him.

17 German *Präsens* in English

1. If the bus doesn't come soon, we'll miss our train. 2. Our train leaves at 10.32. – When does it arrive in Paris? 3. This is your captain speaking. We are flying over / across the (English) Channel at the moment / We are just flying over / across the (English) Channel. We will probably land at London-Heathrow in about 30 minutes. 4. Our luggage is coming. / Here comes our luggage. – Just a moment, I'll get / fetch a trolley. 5. We are going / travelling to Vienna next week. – How long will you be / are you going to be away, then? 6. Ladies and gentlemen, I'm afraid we have a problem with one of the engines. We are going to make an emergency landing. 7. Do you know that Sue lives / is living in London now? – Yes, I've known that for a long time / for ages. She has been working for British Airways for some time. 8. I'll phone / call you as soon as / when we arrive in New York.

18 At Loch Ness

Mr and Mrs Brown are enjoying their holiday in Scotland. They left home three days ago and travelled to Edinburgh, where they spent a couple of nights. Now they have arrived at Loch Ness. Of course they have both heard of the Loch Ness Monster, so they hope the monster will appear while they are there. Twenty minutes ago, they parked their car on / at the edge of the loch, Mr Brown got his camera ready, and (they) both sat down on the grass. But they haven't seen the monster yet. Mrs Brown is getting bored, and they are both beginning to feel hungry. Now they have been waiting for quite a long time, but Mr Brown hasn't given up hope yet. He thinks that perhaps he / they will still see the monster. If it doesn't appear in the next five minutes, they'll have to give up after all.

19 October 1066

On October 1st 1066, only a few days after he had beaten the Norwegians at the Battle of Stamford Bridge in the North of England, Harold heard that William of Normandy had landed on the south coast. Harold and his men were resting at York when the news came. Although he had lost many of his men at Stamford Bridge and those who had survived the battle were now tired, Harold began the march south on October 3rd. He knew that by the time they reached the south coast, they would be exhausted, but there was no alternative. In London, a few reinforcements were waiting to join them as soon as they reached the Thames. By October 13th, the Normans were in sight. Harold's army was probably larger than William's, but the Normans had been resting / had rested for over two weeks, which was / would be an enormous advantage in the battle next day.
October 14th was the decisive day. Until late in the afternoon, it was not clear which side would win the battle. The turning point came when the English, who up to that moment had been fighting from a strong position at the top of a hill, rushed down after the Norman soldiers, who pretended / were pretending / had pretended / had been pretending to run away. When the Normans saw that the English had abandoned their position of strength, they turned back and started

fighting again. Then Harold was hit by an arrow – in the eye. When the English heard / had heard that he and two of his brothers had been killed, they gave up the fight, and the Normans (had) won the day. If Harold and his men had beaten William's army on that autumn day, the future of England would have been very different.

20 Be a green visitor

2. If you do not keep your dog under close control, it will chase the sheep or the cows and they may be frightened. 3. If you do not fasten all gates properly behind you, the animals may escape and run onto the road. 4. If you leave litter, you will spoil the countryside. Litter may even catch fire! 5. If you disturb wild animals or birds, they will be frightened. 6. If you do not leave farm crops and machines alone, you may cause damage and the farmer will get annoyed. 7. If you do not keep to public footpaths across farmland, you will damage the crops. The farmer may get annoyed. 8. If you do not take special care on country roads, you may cause an accident.

21 No problem

2. You would have time for a proper breakfast if you got up twenty minutes earlier. 3. You wouldn't get (so) bored at the weekends if you went out with friends – or joined a club. 4. You wouldn't get through your pocket money so quickly if you planned your spending carefully. 5. You wouldn't have trouble choosing things like clothes and make-up if you took a friend with you to the shops. 6. She wouldn't complain (so much) about the mess in your room if you tidied up regularly. 7. You would remember your friends' birthdays if you wrote them in your diary.

22 How a rainy day can bring you luck

If she hadn't picked up that magazine, she would never have seen the competition on the back page. If it had stopped raining quickly, she wouldn't have stayed in the café, read all the quiz questions and written in the answers. And if the prizes hadn't sounded so good, she would never have taken part in the competition. If she hadn't won that prize and hadn't been interested in tennis she wouldn't have gone to Wimbledon. If it hadn't started to rain or she hadn't forgotten to bring her umbrella, the young man in the seat next to hers wouldn't have shared his umbrella with her, and they wouldn't have got into conversation. And (so) they would never have got to know each other!

23 If things were (or had been) different

2. If they didn't have a dog, going abroad for holidays wouldn't be a problem. 3. If we hadn't taken the wrong exit off the motorway, we wouldn't have arrived late 4. If my father had learnt Latin at school, he would be able to help me with my homework. 5. If that T-shirt hadn't been so expensive, I would have bought it. 6. If Simon had done a paper round, he would have had to get up early in the holidays. 7. If I was / were wearing my glasses, I would be able to read that sign over there. 8. If we didn't have relations in London, we would have stayed at a hotel. 9. If you had asked me to, I would have collected you at the station. 10. If Mum needed the car tonight, Ben wouldn't be allowed to have it.

24 Possible problems – possible solutions
2. If I should be out when you phone, you will / would be able to / can / could always leave a message. 3. If the tickets should be all sold out, we will / would be able to / can / could always go to another show instead. 4. If Sue shouldn't like the CD you've bought her, she will / would be able to / can / could always change it. 5. If it should rain when we have the barbecue, we will / would be able to / can / could always use the grill in the kitchen. 6. If the station car park should be full, we will / would be able to / can / could always try the one behind the post office.

25 On the beach
He: I wish it wasn't / weren't such a long way back to the hotel. I wish / If only I was / were able to read without glasses. I wish I wasn't / weren't so forgetful. If only / I'd rather she didn't always interfere. / I wish she hadn't interfered. I wish / I'd rather she wasn't / weren't so critical.
She: I'd rather he went back and got his glasses. I wish he behaved more sensibly. If only he weren't so forgetful. If only he had remembered his reading glasses.

Chapter 10: The passive voice

1 The worst floods for 40 years
The South East of England has been hit by the worst floods for 40 years. Yesterday, as rivers in Kent burst their banks, **hundreds of people had to be rescued from their homes (by the Army). Some low-lying areas have been flooded** twice already this year. In parts of Sussex, as the water is beginning to subside, **a number of drowned sheep and cattle have been discovered. Many farmers' land and herds have been totally destroyed (by the flooding).** Some say **they could be ruined.**
In Maidstone, Kent, **the River Medway was swelled / swollen by high tides.** Throughout the morning, **hundreds of sandbags were delivered (by the council).** In Yalding **32 adults and 15 children were rescued from their homes (by the fire brigade).** Angela Shave, 45, said, "My husband and I were trapped upstairs with the water level still rising. We were afraid **we would be swept away (by the water)**."
In order to avoid future problems, **building on river banks and flood plains is to be restricted.** Local authorities will normally no longer allow new homes on at-risk sites. The policy's first test will probably be at Ashford, Kent, where **plans for thousands of new homes near the river Stour have already been passed by the local council.** A spokesman for the Environment Agency said, "We hope **the Ashford homes will be built on higher, safer ground.**" Unfortunately, builders prefer to construct on flood plains; because the land there is flat, **it can be developed more cheaply.**

2 The £25 million spaniel
1. They abandoned him. 2. They almost put him down. 3. They value him at £25 million. 4. He has uncovered £25 million worth of drugs / drugs worth / to the value of / with a street value of £25 million in the last four years. 5. They will take them to the Crofts Dog Show next week. 6. Either members of the public donated them, or the Customs and Excise people took them from animal rescue centres. 7. They produce toy items and tease the dogs with them. They hide them in increasingly inaccessible places and gradually impregnate the odours of the drugs into them. 8. Customs and Excise will give him back to his handler, Jenny Wood.

3 Fatal shark attacks in Australia
Yesterday a 49-year-old swimmer was killed by a shark in Australia. The fatal accident happened not far from the popular Cottlesloe beach near the city of Perth. After he had been pulled out of the water, the man died. His left leg had been bitten off. A friend, who dragged the victim to the shore, was bitten on his legs and feet and had to be taken to hospital. The Perth beaches / The beaches of Perth were closed after the fatal accident.
In the space of only six weeks, three men have now become (the) victims of sharks in Australia. At the end of September, a surfer was killed by a great white shark near Adelaide. The 25-year-old honeymooner from New Zealand had been pulled from his surfboard into the depths of the sea only 50 metres away from the shore. His board was found later, but his body disappeared without a trace.
One / A day after the tourist from New Zealand had been killed, a 17-year-old surfer died near Elliston, 450 kilometres west of Adelaide; he was also attacked and killed by a shark.
INFO: On average, less than one fatal shark attack is registered a / per year.

4 Hadrian's Wall
A long-lost section of Hadrian's Wall has been discovered in Newcastle-upon-Tyne. The foundations were found during construction of a public leisure centre. Paul Bidell, head of archaeology at Tyne and Wear Museum, said that 20 yards of the foundations would be restored in the near future. "At the moment the first short stretch is being dug up," he said.
Emperor Hadrian ordered the Wall to be built in 122. In the early 1990s, at *Vindolanda*, a large palace of some 50 rooms was discovered. Recently it has been / was dated to about AD 120, and therefore it is believed to be the headquarters from which the construction of the Wall was supervised / (was being supervised) by the Emperor himself.
The Wall is the most important monument to be built by the Romans in Britain, and it is the best-known frontier in the entire Roman empire. When Hadrian's Wall had been / was completed, it ran for 117 kilometres, from the North Sea to the Irish Sea.
The construction of the Wall was carried out by the three Roman legions in the province. (The idea that the Wall was built by slave labour is wrong.) And modifications were still being made at the time of Hadrian's death in 138.
The province was protected from the "barbarians" in the North and the frontier was controlled. The Wall was guarded by soldiers from the Northern provinces, not

by soldiers from Rome or Italy. Each of the forts on the Wall appears to have been built to hold a regiment of soldiers.
After the legions had been / were ordered back to defend Rome at the beginning of the 5th century, the Wall was left to decay. In the Middle Ages, the Wall was frequently plundered for stones, which were used to build houses and churches.
Today the Wall is looked after by *English Heritage* and is visited by thousands of tourists every year.

5 Crime and other problems
2. The Hunters' house was broken into while they were away on holiday. 3. A window was broken, but I imagine that will be paid for by the insurance. 4. I think hooligans should be dealt with more strictly (by the law). 5. The Palmers last saw their son three weeks ago, and he hasn't been heard of since. 6. There wouldn't be so many dogs in animal rescue centres if they were looked after properly by their owners. 7. Small children and the elderly are often taken unfair advantage of. 8. The details of the case are being looked into very thoroughly (by the police).

6 Saying it differently
2. On the first evening of our holiday, we were shown a film about the island. 3. Have you ever been offered drugs? 4. Lucky you! I've never been given a free ticket for a rock concert! 5. How much are you paid for helping out in the shop? – Not as much as I was first promised! 6. John is going to be offered a part in the play after all. 7. I don't think we'll be sent an invitation to the wedding. 8. Those are nice flowers. – Yes, I was given them on my birthday.

7 What people say
1. She is said / supposed to be the oldest woman in the world / on earth. 2. Some of Shakespeare's sonnets are supposed / believed / said to have been written by other authors. 3. Politicians are known to promise a lot. 4. The bank robbers are thought / believed to have escaped in a friend's car. 5. The Aborigines are supposed / believed / thought to have come to Australia more than 60,000 years ago.

Chapter 11: Auxiliaries

1 *Be, have* or *do*?
1. did – do 2. has been doing – was 3. is – doing – is having 4. Does – doesn't – do 5. Have – done – haven't 6. is – isn't – has been 7. haven't – are being 8. Do – have – do – didn't – was 9. are – having – do

2 Reacting to different situations
2. You can / could / might ring him up. 3. You should / ought to walk when the weather's OK. 4. Can / Could / May / Might I use your telephone? 5. You mustn't smoke (in) here. 6. You needn't show me how to work it / how it works. 7. You shouldn't / oughtn't to stay up so late in the evenings / every night. 8. We may / might miss the bus. 9. That / It must be Sue.

3 Say it with auxiliaries
2. I really **can't** concentrate. 3. You **mustn't** leave a dog locked in a car on a hot day. 4. **Could** you park somewhere else? 5. This **may** be a short cut. 6. My father **can** be very strict. 7. The supermarket on Monks Road **might** still be open. 8. The waiter **couldn't** speak / understand (any) English. 9. You **needn't** call me back.

4 Must? Mustn't? Needn't?
1. needn't 2. must 3. mustn't 4. needn't 5. mustn't 6. needn't 7. must 8. must 9. needn't 10. mustn't

5 Could you be a police officer?
Could you be a police officer? Do you think you would <u>be able to</u> deal with all the situations a police officer <u>has to</u> deal with in his or her job? Or even if you applied, do you think you <u>would be allowed to</u> join the police?
Patsy: I've been with the police for five years. In that time I <u>have had to</u> do a lot of quite difficult things. Yesterday, for example, I <u>had to</u> talk to a 15-year-old schoolgirl. Her boyfriend is a drug dealer. I tried to persuade her to shop him, but she felt she <u>wasn't able to</u> do it. I'm going to <u>have to</u> talk to her again tomorrow. Of course, she's terrified of what he might do to her. But I still hope I <u>will be able to</u> persuade her.
Dave: Last Saturday the police <u>had to</u> deal with some trouble after a football match. This is always difficult. When the fans get violent, we <u>have to</u> try to disperse them calmly. Of course, we <u>aren't allowed to</u> use violence ourselves, but we <u>are allowed to</u> defend ourselves if it gets really rough. On Saturday things were pretty bad, but we <u>were able to</u> restore order eventually. Six blokes <u>had to</u> be arrested, though.
Diane: What do you think it feels like to <u>have to</u> go round to somebody's house and tell a woman that her husband and two children have been killed in a car crash? I <u>had to</u> do that last week. At first I thought I <u>wouldn't be able to</u> do it. I was glad there was another officer with me, so I <u>didn't have to</u> go alone.
Jack: Each year, about 35,000 people apply for a job with the police, but only about 5,000 <u>are allowed to</u> join. You <u>have to</u> be very fit, for one thing. If you apply but you aren't fit enough, you <u>aren't allowed to</u> join the police. Would you <u>be able to</u> chase a shoplifter up the stairs of a tower block, for example? <u>Being able to</u> do things like that is vital in the police force. People who <u>aren't able to</u> pass the medical <u>have to</u> be turned down. Of course, there are other qualities we <u>have to</u> look out for apart from physical fitness. <u>Being able to</u> observe and remember the details of scenes accurately is very important, for example. A police officer also <u>has to</u> <u>be able to</u> behave sensitively ...

6 Will you help me, please?
2. He won't eat any dog biscuits. 3. She doesn't / won't want to pay so much. / She isn't / won't be willing / won't be prepared to pay so much. 4. I'll shut the window. 5. It won't start in cold weather. 6. Will / Would you dial for me? 7. ... but he wouldn't / didn't want to / refused to give it to me. 8. Will / Would you help me translate it? 9. I won't have my hair cut. 10. I would like to live in a

warmer country. 11. But he won't / doesn't want to / refuses to see a doctor. 12. We have always wanted to go there.

7 Life used to be quite different then

... Damals hatten wir kein heißes Wasser, das aus einem Wasserhahn kam, wann immer man es brauchte / wollte. Jeden Samstagnachmittag brachte meine Mutter einen großen Topf Wasser auf dem Herd zum Kochen und goss es in eine große Wanne in der Küche. Dann stiegen wir Kinder in die Wanne – einer nach dem anderen – und wir benutzten natürlich alle dasselbe Wasser. Wie würde dir das gefallen, Tommy? Wenn man sich erst einmal daran gewöhnt hat, jeden Tag warm zu duschen, vergisst man natürlich, wie es damals war. Nach dem Bad legte uns meine Mutter frische Kleider hin – und sie reichten uns (immer) die ganze Woche. Sonntags gingen wir (immer) in die Kirche, und natürlich mussten wir unsere Kleider bis dahin sauber halten. Ja, wir spielten auch Fußball. Oft hatten wir keinen richtigen Ball, deshalb benutzten wir stattdessen eine alte Dose, oder sogar einen Stein. Und damals war / gab es kaum Verkehr, deshalb spielten wir oft auf der Hauptstraße Fußball. Das wäre heute schwierig, nicht wahr? Manchmal erzählte *mein* Großvater *mir*, wie das Leben war, als er ein Junge war. Aber wenn ich dir das erzählen würde, Tommy, würdest du es nicht glauben.

8 Shall we? Are we supposed to?

2. People / They should share (their cars) or use public transport. 3. We should have / ought to have filled the tank before. 4. Shall we switch the TV on? 5. We're supposed to do exercises 3 to 8. 6. Are we supposed to bring food and drinks? 7. It was supposed to (have) come at 9 o'clock. 8. I should / ought to make an appointment.

9 You should have ...

2. You needn't have waited. 3. You should have watched it (with me). 4. He must have gone by bus after all. 5. So we needn't have worried. 6. You should have asked (me). 7. There must have been an accident. 8. I should have apologized. 9. We needn't have booked seats. 10. We must have taken the wrong turning at that roundabout.

10 Do you need some more time?

2. b + H 3. e + E 4. d + A 5. c + B 6. f + I 7. i + G 8. g + D 9. h + F

Chapter 12: The verb and its objects

1 Words that can easily be confused
1. raise 2. lay 3. set 4. lying 5. lay 6. sit 7. rise 8. sat 9. raised 10. laid 11. rose 12. set

2 What's that in German?
1. Kent wird der Garten Englands genannt, weil dort so viel Obst angebaut wird. 2. Ben ist sehr gewachsen, seit ich ihn zum letzten mal gesehen habe. 3. Ich weiß leider nicht, wie man diesen Kartenautomaten bedient. 4. Ich habe eine neue Batterie in meinen Wecker eingesetzt, aber er funktioniert immer noch nicht. 5. Du solltest / Man sollte das Wasser nicht laufen lassen, während du dir / man sich die Zähne putzt. 6. Es war schon immer der Traum meines Vaters, ein Fünfsternehotel zu leiten / führen.

3 Using phrasal verbs
a) 1. get off 2. put – away 3. look after 4. take – away 5. put – up – putting off 6. got over 7. looking round 8. Look out 9. taken – out 10. taken over 11. get on
b) 1. take your coat off / take off your coat 2. pick her up 3. Look at it 4. look it up 5. put you through 6. take the rubbish out / take out the rubbish 7. Throw it away 8. put my appointment off / put off my appointment

4 Overheard at school
2. me your biro 3. it to Mike 4. three or four of you a lift 5. our guests some textbooks 6. them to the people in the back row 7. them to those that haven't seen them yet 8. a second piece to the people that have only had one

5 Tuesday
… In the morning Sam said good-bye to his wife. When he got to his office, he gave a kiss to Naomi, his favourite secretary / Naomi, his favourite secretary, a kiss. Then he dictated to her a few business letters to their partners in South America / (a few business letters to their partners in South America to her). That only took them about half an hour. Then he drove downtown to buy his wife a $50.000 bracelet / a $50.000 bracelet for his wife, a little birthday present. When he got back, his second-in-command introduced a group of Japanese businessmen to him / to him a group of Japanese businessmen / him to a group of Japanese businessmen. Naomi offered all of them glasses of champagne / glasses of champagne to all of them, and Sam started to describe the functions of the new Super-PC to his guests, explaining all the advantages to them. He mentioned the possibility of an evening out together, and they smiled politely when he suggested this to them. In the afternoon, he met with some trade union officials and announced to them the firm's decision to lay off another 2000 workers / (the firm's decision to lay off another 2000 workers to them). He explained the reasons for these cuts to the angry officials and promised all of the workers the firm's generous help / the firm's generous help to all of the workers. At last he was able to show his Japanese

friends some of the city's sizzling nightlife / some of the city's sizzling nightlife to his Japanese friends. The next morning his wife asked her husband some questions about his workday, but Sam didn't mention all the details to her.

6 Your opinion, please!

Possible answers:

1. I consider global warning (as) a great problem. 2. I regard computer games as a waste of time. 3. I would describe most politicians as honest. 4. I look upon nuclear power as dangerous. 5. I consider genetically modified products (as) problematic. 6. I accept women in the armed forces as normal. 7. I would call extreme sports crazy. 8. I find smoking unnecessary / perfectly acceptable. 9. I find science fiction films boring. 10. I think job-sharing a good idea.

7 Laughter really seems to be the best medicine

Laughter, the best medicine

The research report of a group of American doctors confirms an old saying: laughter really seems to be the best medicine. The doctors claim that people who like / enjoy watching funny videos are sure / certain to have fewer heart attacks than others. They have also discovered / found out that people with heart problems generally laugh less. Such people don't seem to recognize the humour in many situations, and this is likely to have a negative effect on their health.

"I'm afraid we still don't know exactly in what way / how laughing protects the heart," explained Dr Eric Miller, the well-known heart specialist / Dr Miller ... explained. "But the reasons are likely to be discovered soon. (A Canadian team happens to be working on the same question, too.)"

"We know that people who exercise, don't smoke and eat lowfat food are sure / certain to reduce the risk of (having) a heart attack. And I hope people will add daily laughter to that list, too."

So if you want to live to be a hundred, go on / keep (on) enjoying those stupid / silly videos you used to watch secretly.

Chapter 13: The infinitive

1 What do they expect?
2. Jessica's parents ask / expect / want her to tell them who she is going out with. 3. The police warn / advise people never to leave bicycles unlocked. 4. My driving instructor tells / warns me not to drive too fast near schools and playgrounds. 5. Jack's sister asks / expects /warns / tells / wants him to ask her before he borrows her things. 6. Our neighbours ask / expect / want us to keep our music low while their baby is sleeping. 7. Tim's mother doesn't expect him to help her in the kitchen. 8. Our coach advises / warns / tells us not to eat too much before a match.

2 What's *dass* in English?
1. We're going to the zoo tomorrow, and we'd like you to come with us. 2. You / One can't expect the lions to roar all the time / the whole time. 3. I'm still waiting for the polar bear to jump / dive into the water. 4. It is important for the animals to be fed regularly. 5. In my opinion it's wrong for animals to be kept in captivity. 6. The chimpanzees are not close / near enough for us to (be able to) photograph them / to take photos / a photo of them. 7. This monkey (here) wants me to give him my banana.

3 Easy for you to do!
2. I'm afraid it's just not possible for me to come to Scotland with you. 3. It's quite unusual for American tourists to come to this part of the world. 4. It's normal for the weather to be windy here at this time of year. 5. Will it be all right for us to visit you in August? 6. There's no need for you to ring us up while you're away. 7. Here's a key for you to use if we should be out.

4 Tips from a teenage magazine
1. make – makes 2. let 3. make – let 4. make – let 5. let – made / making 6. let – make – let

5 Perception and observation
1. saw / noticed her leave 2. hear it ring 3. saw / watched / noticed him take 4. watch them play 5. hear / notice you come in 6. noticed / saw you give 7. feel / notice it touch – felt it sting me

6 The Perfect English School
2. when to use the simple past and when (to use) the present perfect 3. where to put the adverbs in a sentence 4. how to avoid making mistakes 5. whether to say "look nice" or "look nicely" 6. how to learn to speak fluent English 7. where to put commas 8. how to prepare for your exams

7 The way to start a class war?

In the past, if Americans wanted to see identically dressed schoolchildren, **Britain was the country to go to.** This is no longer so. Today, the school round the block is the school **to look at.**

Long Beach in California was the first district **to pioneer school uniforms.** And Philadelphia is the first big city **to make uniforms obligatory in all its schools.** But it is no longer the only one **to ask parents to buy uniforms for their children.**

So for many American parents, school uniform will soon be the most expensive item **to buy for school.** Poor inner-city Americans are not the only people **to complain about this new trend.**

Kate Singleton, 16-year-old high school student, says: "In Britain school uniforms are traditionally worn **(in order) to disguise social differences.** But here in America everybody is free and equal, and school uniforms would be the best way **to kill creativity and individuality.** I'll be the last person **ever to wear those Mickey Mouse costumes.**"

But many students disagree. For them wearing school uniform is a good way **to show a sense of identity and commitment to the school.**

So, as with so many disputes in America, the courts may be the place **to decide this question.**

8 To tell the truth ...

Moderator: Und hier ist wieder „Im Brennpunkt". Wir wollen zuerst einmal unsere Gäste heute Abend begrüßen: Sue Pendleton von der Labour Party und Michael Atkinson von den Konservativen. Natürlich ist das Ergebnis dieser Debatte völlig offen, und es bleibt abzuwarten ...

Sue: Also, ehrlich gesagt, das was Michael über unsere Politik gesagt hat, entspricht nicht den Tatsachen. Ich bin die letzte, die nahelegen / andeuten / suggerieren würde, dass solche Dinge unter den Teppich gekehrt werden sollten. Und um fair zu sein, es gab anscheinend ein paar – hm – Missverständnisse. Es ist zu erwarten, dass ...

Michael: Es tut mir leid, Susan, aber Sie haben uns anscheinend völlig missverstanden. Um die Wahrheit zu sagen, Ihre Partei versucht immer, die Zahlen in einem besseren Licht erscheinen zu lassen. Aber im Großen und Ganzen wollen die Wähler, dass die Parteien ihnen die Wahrheit sagen. Also, kurz und gut, ...

Sue: Zu behaupten, wir würden die Wähler anlügen, ist eine Beleidigung. Und ich warte darauf / erwarte, dass Michael sich dafür entschuldigt. Er wird wahrscheinlich nie verstehen, wie die Wirklichkeit aussieht. Man muss sich nur umschauen, um zu sehen, wie schlimm die Dinge geworden sind. Aber ich bin nicht die Einzige, die bemerkt / erkannt hat ...

Moderator: Ich muss sie beide leider hier unterbrechen. Zusammenfassend danke ich Ihnen beiden für die lebendige / lebhafte und informative Diskussion. Unsere beiden Kandidaten haben Ihnen die Entscheidung bei den nächsten Wahlen bestimmt erleichtert. „Im Brennpunkt" ist *die* Sendung für politisch Interessierte / *die* Sendung, die politisch Interessierte anschauen sollten. Gute Nacht.

Chapter 14: The gerund

1 Tiger Woods

Possible answers: They were not keen on non-whites mixing with the spectators. They were afraid of people objecting. They were afraid of some of their members complaining. They were against blacks coming into the club house. They hated the idea of trouble starting (at the club). They were afraid of some members leaving the club. They didn't like / hated the idea of their old traditions changing.

2 Ever tried surfing?

Lucy: We couldn't wait to get into the water! But actually, if you mean to learn how to surf properly, you need to start with the "dry land basics". That means checking the sea for jetties or rocks. And you mustn't forget to check there's no red flag flying – that tells you it's dangerous to surf or (to) swim.

Tom: Before we started on our first day, we had to practise on the beach, with our boards on the sand. Quite a few people stopped to watch us, we must have looked so funny! We tried to do everything right, and soon our instructor said we could try practising in the water. I'll never forget trying to stand up on the board the first time. Impossible! I thought I'd never learn! But I didn't stop practising. Soon we all started to improve /improving.

Sophie: When you get on the board, you must remember to keep your knees bent. Not easy! But the most difficult thing is trying to judge when the wave is going to break. I can remember practising again and again before I succeeded! Our instructor is fabulous – and the course has been really great. I'll never regret coming here and taking part.

3 The problem of phobias

… Do you **start sweating** when you **imagine going up** an escalator? In Britain alone there are millions of people with phobias, who **worry about having to do** things that other people do not find frightening at all.

Some people **can't stand looking** at raw meat. Others **hate being** in a dark place. **This can mean being unable** to spend the night away from home in case they cannot find a light switch.

Michelle's case is typical; she **started feeling frightened** of escalators when she was a small child. Twenty years later this fear turned into a phobia. At first she **avoided going** by tube. Then she **stopped going** to any places where there might be a lot of stairs. "Even **when I dreamed /dreamt of going** on an escalator, I woke up shaking all over," she says. "In the end I needed treatment."

Lots of people like Michelle **rely on taking** drugs. But if they **go on taking** pills over a long period, they may **end up becoming addicted.** Doctors **insist on their patients / patients' facing** their fears. A specialist at one of Britain's treatment centres says: "When once you have **succeeded in letting** that hairy spider run up your arm, you have beaten your particular phobia and you can **look forward to leading** a normal life again."

4 The idea of sunbathing

2. But in those days people weren't keen on lying in the sun. 3. A dark skin was associated with low class. This was because the only people that were used to working outside were peasants. 4. By the 1920s rich Americans were crazy about going to the fashionable South of France. 5. And back home they were proud of showing off their suntan – now a status symbol for the rich. 6. Today we have got used to seeing millions of sunbathers on European beaches. 7. On those beaches, people have the opportunity of dropping some of their everyday boundaries, like shyness or social class. 8. And today nobody feels ashamed of dropping all their clothes, too. 9. But in some places – like Brazil or the US –the idea of going topless is out of the question. 10. And in many hot countries, people have difficulty in understanding how anyone can lie in the heat for hours on end. 11. Today, with the shrinking of the ozone layer, people realize the danger of being in the sun too long. 12. So perhaps in the future, people will get tired of lying in the sun to get a suntan because they are afraid of getting skin cancer.

5 Please don't feed the wildlife

Wir als Besucher spielen eine genauso große Rolle, wenn es darum geht, unsere Nationalparks in Ordnung zu halten, wie die Verwalter der Nationalparks. Das Füttern von (wilden) Tieren ist ein klassisches Beispiel dafür, wie gute Absichten das ökologische Gleichgewicht stören können.
Es ist schon lange bekannt, dass Tiere sich schnell daran gewöhnen, von Menschen gefüttert zu werden. Aber wenn sie erst einmal gewohnt sind, menschliche Nahrung zu sich zu nehmen, enthalten die Mägen der Tiere nur diejenigen Bakterien, die zur Verdauung menschlicher Nahrung nötig sind. Wenn die Touristensaison endet und der Winter beginnt, haben diese Tiere Schwierigkeiten, überhaupt Nahrung zu finden, oder – wenn sie welche finden – sind sie in Gefahr, mit vollem Magen zu verhungern.
Was noch schlimmer ist, das Füttern kann dazu führen, dass normalerweise sanftmütige Tiere wie Hirsche und Rehe aggressiv werden. In einem bestimmten, traurigen Fall wurde ein kleines Kind von einem Rehbock getötet, als es sein belegtes Brot selbst essen wollte, statt es dem Tier zu geben.
Natürlich füttern Kinder gern diese niedlichen Tiere, aber wenn man auch nur ein einziges Mal den großen, braunen, flehenden Augen nachgibt, kann es tragische Folgen haben. Seien Sie verantwortungsbewusst! Lernen Sie, ein Tierfreund zu sein, indem Sie nicht versuchen, sich durch Futter mit Tieren anzufreunden.

6 On patrol at a London school

A school in London has now become the first to copy America by having its own police officer. Police Constable Andy Briers, 34, has now got his office at Northumberland Park School, in one of London's toughest areas. In one incident last term, four teenage girls not from the school came into the building with two enormous kitchen knives; **in another case a boy nearly died after being attacked by fellow pupils. Apart from sending off gangs of intruders, PC Briers also makes truancy patrols and sends pupils back to lessons / PC Briers sends off gangs of intruders, as well as making truancy patrols and sending pupils back to lessons. He has been with the police for seven years as well as being a quali-**

fied PE teacher / Apart from having been with the police for seven years, he is a qualified PE teacher, too.
So far he has had a good influence on the school, and the staff accept him. **He has been there for a few weeks now without having had to arrest a pupil at all.** "You can sort out most problems at school," he said. **"But I would arrest pupils for bringing weapons to school or taking drugs."**
In spite of being disliked by some pupils, he is already on first-name terms with many. Thanassi, 18, from a Greek family, said: "Security has improved a lot. And we really like Andy." **His presence builds people's confidence in the police instead of being seen as a threat / Instead of being seen as a threat, his presence builds people's confidence in the police.**

7 How about doing this exercise?
2. What / How about eating out? 3. It's not worth / It's no use / It's no good waiting. 4. It's no use / it's no good phoning her now. 5. There's no / It's no use denying it. 6. There's no knowing 7. It's worth booking seats. / What / How about booking seats? 8. It's worth going there. / What / How about going there?

Chapter 15: Participles

1 Stay switched on, please
1. stood waiting / were standing waiting 2. sits watching 3. lying stretched out 4. remain closed 5. stay chatting 6. went crashing 7. comes running 8. stay connected

2 Experiences
1. standing – take / taking – come – knock 2. get / getting – bump – pushing – open – slipping 3. come – playing – screech – drive – screaming 4. getting – lengthening – setting – singing – appear

3 What's that in English?
1. Your hair looks super! – Thanks! I had / got it cut yesterday. 2. Why don't you have / get your old bike repaired? 3. Shall I close the window? – No, let's leave it open for a while. 4. Our teachers make us work pretty hard. 5. Sandra (has) left her camera on the bus. 6. What was the matter? / What was wrong? Why did you keep us waiting so long? 7. Please let us know if you want to accept the offer. 8. Would you like to take off your jacket / to take your jacket off? – No, thanks, I'll keep it on. 9. I'm afraid these trousers aren't washable. I always have to have / get them cleaned. 10. We (have) left the dog at home today. But he didn't want to let us go at first.

4 The new Americans
In the 19th century, America was an enormous magnet, **which drew** people into it from every direction. There were two distinct waves of immigrants **who / that**

entered the US. The first phase, **which lasted** until about 1880, is called the "old immigration". Most of those immigrants were farmers, **who (had) often left** behind poverty or famine. These people, **who were attracted** by the availability of land, settled mainly in the Midwest and the Great Plains.
In the 1880s, there came another wave of immigrants, **which was known** as the "new immigration". These immigrants were mostly Catholics and Jews **who / that came / had come** from southern and eastern Europe.
The new immigrants – **who were encouraged** by new immigration laws, by the new steamship service **that / which had been opened** between America and Europe and by letters **that / which were / had been sent** from people who had gone before – moved to the US in search of greater economic opportunity. The excitement **that / which was felt** by immigrants **who came** to the New World was mixed with anxiety and fear. The immigrants **who / that landed** in New York had to pass through the immigration centre on Ellis Island, **which had been set** up by the federal government in 1892. These newcomers, **who brought / were bringing** with them the various cultures of Europe, broadened the cultural life of American cities. One of those immigrants was a composer, **who was / had been born** in Russia and **(was) named** Baline. Baline, **who is / was better known** as Irving Berlin, expressed his love for his new country in patriotic songs, **which include** "God Bless America".

5 Robinson Crusoe
"Robinson Crusoe" is a novel by Daniel Defoe **published in 1719. Although later taking on** an almost mythological status, **the novel** is based on a true story, **written** by A. S. Selkirk. Selkirk was a sailor **put ashore** on an uninhabited island in 1704 **and managing to survive** until his rescue in 1709.
It seems probable that Daniel Defoe got the idea for his book **after meeting / having met** Selkirk in 1711.
In Defoe's story, Crusoe, a young man, goes to sea **though (having been) warned** by his parents / ... Crusoe, a young man, **though (having been) warned** by his parents, goes to sea. He suffers a number of misfortunes **until (being) finally / finally being shipwrecked** off South America.
After living / having lived on the island for 28 years, he is finally rescued. **While staying** on the island, Crusoe adapts to his alien environment, **demonstrating** the self-sufficiency **admired** so much by Defoe himself. **Combining** typical characteristics of the adventure story and fascinating aspects of travel literature, the novel was an instant success. It has become one of the classics of English literature, **enjoyed** by both young and adult readers.

6 The "Boston Massacre" – 5 March 1770
a) **After / When / As British troops had been sent** to defend British customs officials, the mood in Boston was tense and ugly. **When / After / As the rumour had spread** that British soldiers had beaten up two Boston youths, an angry crowd gathered. Some Bostonians threw snowballs and sticks at a small contingent of British soldiers. **When / After one soldier had been struck** by a stick and **(had been) thrown** to the ground, the others panicked and started to fire into the mass of civilians. In half a minute the street was empty – **the dead and**

wounded had been left on the ground. Three Americans had been killed outright – among them Crispus Atticus, a runaway slave – **and two others later died** of their wounds. The authorities promised to punish those responsible for the "Boston Massacre". **As a jury found** the commander of the soldiers innocent, only two soldiers were arrested and branded on the thumb with the letter "M" – for manslaughter. But the British withdrew from Boston. **When / After / Once the hated army had gone,** the mood in Boston improved. Until the next incident: the Boston Tea Party.

b) Nachdem britische Truppen geschickt worden waren, um britische Zollbeamte zu verteidigen, war die Stimmung in Boston angespannt und unangenehm. Als sich das Gerücht verbreitet hatte, britische Soldaten hätten zwei junge Männer aus Boston zusammengeschlagen, versammelte sich eine wütende Menge. Einige Bostoner bewarfen ein kleines Kontingent britischer Soldaten mit Schneebällen und Stöcken. Als einer der Soldaten von einem Stock getroffen und zu Boden geworfen wurde, gerieten die anderen in Panik und begannen, in die Menge der Zivilisten zu schießen. Innerhalb einer halben Minute war die Straße leer – die Toten und Verwundeten waren auf dem Boden liegen gelassen worden. Drei Amerikaner waren auf der Stelle getötet worden – darunter Crispus Atticus, ein entlaufener Sklave –, und zwei weitere starben später an ihren Verletzungen. Die Behörden versprachen, die für das „Massaker von Boston" Verantwortlichen zu bestrafen. Da ein Gericht den Befehlshaber der Soldaten für unschuldig befand, wurden nur zwei Soldaten festgenommen und mit dem Buchstaben „M" – für „manslaughter" („Totschlag") – auf dem Daumen gebrandmarkt. Aber die Briten zogen sich aus Boston zurück. Als die verhasste Armee abgezogen war, verbesserte sich die Stimmung in Boston. Bis zum nächsten Vorfall, der „Boston Tea Party".

Chapter 16: Subordinate clauses

1 George Washington

2. i 3. f 4. h 5. b 6. a 7. c 8. j 9. d 10. e

2 Into space

1. The first artificial satellite, which was called "Sputnik 1", went into orbit round the Earth in 1957. / The first artificial satellite that / which went into orbit round the Earth in 1957 was called "Sputnik 1".
2. The Russian Yuri Gagarin, who made one orbit of the Earth in 1961, was the first person to go up into space. / The Russian Yuri Gagarin, who was the first person to go up into space, made one orbit of the Earth in 1961.
3. The moon is a hostile place that / which has no atmosphere to keep the temperatures constant. / The moon, which has no atmosphere to keep the temperatures constant, is a hostile place. / The moon, which is a hostile place, has no atmosphere to keep the temperatures constant.
4. Great plains stretch over the moon, whose surface / the surface of which is dotted with huge mountains and craters.

5. The moon, which we can only see because it acts like a huge mirror reflecting / that / which refects light from the sun, has no light of its own. / We can only see the moon, which has no light of its own, because it acts like a huge mirror reflecting / that / which refects light from the sun.
6. Over the years scientists have often tried to explain the formation of the moon, for which they have produced many theories.
7. Some have suggested that the moon may have originally been part of the Earth, a piece of which / of which a piece may have broken off millions of years ago.
8. Neil Armstrong, whom Americans are proud to remember as the first person to set foot on the moon, was one of the crew of the Apollo 11 spacecraft. / Americans are proud to remember Neil Armstrong, who was one of the crew of the Apollo 11 spacecraft, as the first person to set foot on the moon.
9. Huge distances, which are simply impossible for us to imagine, separate our solar system from others. / The huge distances that separate our solar system from the others are simply impossible for us to imagine.
10. If you could travel by plane to Proxima Centauri, (which is) the nearest star to our own solar system, it would mean a long journey that / which would take two million years. / If you could travel by plane to Proxima Centauri, (which is) the nearest star to our own solar system, which would take two million years, it would mean a long journey.
11. Our galaxy alone contains about 100 billion stars, all of which / of which all may have their own huge solar systems.
12. Our galaxy, which is called the Milky Way, is an independent system of stars existing / that / which exist together in space. / Our galaxy, which is an independent system of stars existing / that / which exist together in space, is called the Milky Way.

3 Explaining what words mean

1. An exercise book is a book you write exercises in. 2. A garage is a building you keep your car in. (It is also a place cars are repaired at or a place you can buy petrol at.) 3. A microwave is an oven you can quickly heat or cook food in. 4. A stranger is a person you don't know / you haven't met before. 5. A backpack is a bag you carry on your back. 6. A ticket machine is a machine you can get tickets from. 7. Primary school is the school British children go to from the age of five until the age of eleven. 8. Rent is the money you have to pay for living in a flat or house. 9. A youth hostel is a place young people can stay at. 10. Your mother tongue is the language you first learn to speak as a child. 11. A toothbrush is a small brush you clean your teeth with. 12. Your homework is the work your teacher tells you to do at home. 13. Chopsticks are things Chinese people eat their food with. 14. Your favourite book is the book you like best. 15. A mobile phone is a phone you can carry around with you to telephone wherever you are. 16. A vacuum cleaner is a machine / a thing / an appliance you clean floors / carpets with.

4 Less formal, please!

1. Please let me see those photos (which / that) you are looking at. 2. Look, that's the house (which / that) we once lived in. 3. Sarah is the girl (who / that) you saw me playing tennis with yesterday. 4. I don't think I've ever met the people (who / that) you were talking about just now. 5. Where's the farm shop (which / that) you

always get your vegetables from? 6. The 17th century is the period of history (which / that) I'm especially interested in. 7. The Jacksons? Are they the ones (who / that) you sent a card to when we were in Greece? 8. Luckily, the weather is still something (which / that) we have no control over.

5 Working on Christmas Day

Sandra Brook, who is 28, is a nurse who / that works in the Accident and Emergency Department of a west London hospital. Unlike most of the people (who / that) she knows, Sandra will be working on Christmas Day – from 8 a.m. to 8.30 p.m. It will not be the first Christmas Day (which / that) she has spent working. Given the choice of working either over Christmas or the New Year, Sandra, whose parents live in Canada and whose closest friends will be spending the day with their families, has decided on the former, which will mean that she will be free to celebrate the New Year with friends.

Sandra expects to be fairly busy on Christmas Day. "Illness and accidents aren't things which / that just stop at Christmas!" she says. "GPs' surgeries will be closed, of course, so people won't be able to go to the doctor (who / that) they're used to. That means we'll see a few people who / that have burnt their fingers on pots and pans while cooking the Christmas lunch. People of other religions who /which /that don't celebrate Christmas may also come in because it's just a day like any other to them." The thing (which / that) Sandra finds hardest to bear is when people die at Christmas. "I feel so sorry for the families because of the time of the year. But the saddest thing (which / that) I've experienced is the number of people in hospital whose relatives don't visit them – or who / that have no family at all." The nurses try to take extra time to talk to patients who / that are obviously alone, and to help them join in the festivities. Gifts are donated to the hospital, which ensures that nobody feels forgotten.

Does Sandra feel annoyed about having to work over Christmas? "Not at all. The good thing about this job is that you know you're helping people who / that are in pain or distress. – And there's the evening (which / that) I can look forward to. I'll be spending it with my boyfriend, John."

6 On holiday in Scotland

a) 2. which makes it hard to understand people. 3. which is an advantage, of course. 4. which means that I certainly won't go swimming. 5. which means we don't get much sleep. 6. which makes him pretty boring. 7. which makes it very difficult to get there at night. 8. which I find far too much effort.

b) Possible answers: 1. which means that I won't have to go to school on that day! 2. which is really fantastic! 3. which is worrying him a lot / which is very annoying for him. 4. which meant she was late for school this morning.

7 Whatever you say

1. whatever 2. whatever 3. Whoever 4. Whichever 5. whichever 6. whoever

Chapter 17: Statements, questions, shortened sentences

1 Surely not!
2. Wales isn't part of England. (It's part of Great Britain / the United Kingdom.) 3. Shakespeare wasn't born in London. (He was born in Stratford-on-Avon.) 4. Daniel Defoe didn't write "Treasure Island". (Robert Louis Stevenson wrote it. / Daniel Defoe wrote "Robinson Crusoe".) 5. James Bond doesn't work for the FBI. (He works for Her Majesty's Secret Service.) 6. At the end of the Industrial Revolution no one in England had a car. 7. The Winter Olympic Games have never been held in Scotland. 8. The Irish don't drive on the right. (They drive on the left.) 9. Today no prisoners are kept in the Tower of London. 10. None of the famous Boat Races on the Thames has been won by Manchester University. (They have all been won either by Oxford or by Cambridge University.) 11. "Nessie" hasn't been caught and can't be seen in London Zoo. 12. Black Americans aren't called "Native Americans". (American Indians are called "Native Americans". / Black Americans are called "African Americans".) 13. Henry VIII didn't have eight wives. (He only had six wives.) 14. The Indians didn't have horses before Columbus discovered America. (The Spanish brought horses to America.)

2 Do not enter
1. Don't feed the monkey(s). 2. Let's buy / have an ice cream. 3. Take a seat. / Sit down, please. 4. Don't walk on the grass. 5. Don't touch the fence. 6. Let's watch this programme / film. / Let's switch the TV on.

3 Getting to know the neighbours
2. Are the man and the woman married? 3. Isn't their daughter called Jeanette? 4. Does she go to the comprehensive school? 5. Doesn't the father work in Brussels? 6. Didn't they live in France before? 7. Isn't the mother French? 8. Does she speak any English? 9. Don't they have a car? / Haven't they got a car? 10. Do they have a dog? / Have they got a dog? 11. Are they members of the tennis club? 12. Did they paint their house themselves? It looks awful! 13. Am I (being) too nosy?

4 Henry VIII
2. Since when / How long had he been married to Katharine of Aragon? 3. Whose wife had she been before she married Henry? 4. Why did Henry want a divorce from Katharine many years later? 5. Who refused to grant Henry the divorce? 6. How much of the land in England did the Catholic Church own? 7. How did Henry manage to get his divorce? 8. Whose power had come to an end in England now? 9. How many wives did Henry have? 10. How many of his wives were executed? How many of them were divorced? How many died while still married to Henry? Which one / Which of them survived him?

5 *Which, what* or *who*?
1. What 2. Which 3. What 4. Who 5. What – what 6. Which 7. Which 8. Who 9. What 10. Which

6 Your dog doesn't bite, does it?
1. haven't you – I have 2. isn't it – it isn't 3. do you – I do 4. doesn't he – he doesn't 5. didn't you – I did 6. is he – he isn't 7. shall we – let's 8. will you – I will 9. can he – he can 10. won't you – I will

7 Do you agree?
1. So am I 2. Nor / Neither have I 3. I did 4. So did I 5. I didn't 6. So have I 7. Nor / Neither have I 8. Nor / Neither do I 9. So would I

Chapter 18: From sentence to text (linking and emphasis)

1 Falling to the Earth from 12,000 feet
1. It was the last day of my skydiving training course in California, and it was my 27th jump, <u>but</u> I was still scared! It had been an intense week, <u>for</u> I had been constantly confronted with my terrible fear of heights; <u>however</u>, I wouldn't have missed it for the world. 2. Stepping out of a plane two miles up in the air is <u>neither</u> pleasant <u>nor</u> easy. <u>Nevertheless</u>, I somehow managed to live with my fear. I found the best way was to step out quickly; <u>for</u> I realized that I <u>either</u> had to act fast <u>or</u> I wouldn't be able to act at all! I soon got used to it <u>anyway</u>, <u>yet</u> my fear was always there with me. 3. Actually, there is no *real* need to feel worried <u>or</u> scared; <u>after all</u>, you have two instructors firmly holding onto you at the beginning, <u>therefore</u> you are in safe hands. They make sure you pull your ripcord at the right height, <u>and</u> they help you to get into the right "flying" position, <u>too</u>. Then, after 45 seconds of "free fall", your parachute opens <u>and</u> (with a bit of luck) you land gently on the ground! 4. Learning to skydive in California rather than back home in Britain has advantages and disadvantages. <u>On the one hand</u>, the weather is so much better, <u>so</u> you can be sure to finish the course in a week; <u>on the other hand</u>, it costs a lot more. The price includes the flight to Los Angeles, <u>though</u>, <u>and</u> it <u>also</u> includes the hotel, transport from the airport, <u>and</u> so on.

2 Can you do this, too?
1. also 2. also – as well 3. too 4. either 5. too

3 At the beach
There are two children sitting on a blanket / towel, playing cards.
There's a man lying on his back, with a book on his face.
There are a man and a woman sitting on chairs, reading newspapers.
There's a man selling ice cream.

There are a woman and a girl wanting to buy ice cream(s) / talking to the man selling ice cream.
There's a towel laid out on the sand, with a book and a mobile phone (left) on it.
There are three children playing ball on the beach.
There are three children building sandcastles.
There's a boy sitting on a rock, fishing.
There are some fish jumping out of the water.
There's a bucket and spade next to the rock.
There's a couple going into the water, holding hands.
There are three people windsurfing.
There are a boy and a girl swimming.
There's a girl running into the water.
There's a boy pushing a rowing boat into the water.
There's a dog running over the beach towards the sea / running after the boy with the boat.
There are two seagulls flying over the beach.
There's a man sailing.
There's another sailing boat further out.
There are two cars parked on the beach.

4 What's wrong here?
2. No, it was George Washington who / that was the first American president. 3. No, it was in 1492 that he sailed to America. 4. No, it was the east coast of Australia that James Cook claimed for Britain (in 1770). 5. No, it was at the Battle of Waterloo that he was finally defeated (in 1815). 6. No, it was World War II that started in 1939. 7 No, it was the Norwegian Amundsen who / that won the "race" to the South Pole. 8. No, it was on their way back that they died. 9. No, it was Queen Elizabeth I, "the Virgin Queen", that it was called after. 10. No, it was the Russians who / that were the first to send a man into space.

5 Do
1. I did learn my words. 2. I do like your new hairstyle. / Your new hairstyle does look great. 3. Do take a seat. / Do sit down, please. 4. I did enjoy the concert yesterday. 5. I do want to help you. 6. Do be quiet. / Do stop making that awful noise.

6 Journey across Australia
1. Hardly had the expedition left Melbourne in August 1860, when trouble started. 2. Not only did Burke, the leader, know almost nothing about big exditions, but he was also a very impatient man. 3. At first there were 16 men. But scarcely had they gone about a quarter of the way, when nine of them returned to Melbourne. 4. Not only had quarrelling started among the men, but some of them were too slow for Burke. 5. Not until the Australian summer began in November did Burke and the others begin to feel that they had chosen the wrong time of year for the expedition. 6. Because of the terrible heat, Burke and Wills took only two others the rest of the way north. But no sooner did they see / had they seen the Gulf of Carpentaria in front of them, than they realized they could not reach the sea because the land in

between was all swamp! 7. Never in all their lives had the men felt so disappointed. 8. On the way back, heavy rain came down every day. Not only did the terrible weather slow them down, but they all became dangerously ill. 9. Then their food began to run out, and within a few weeks Burke and Wills and one of the other men had died. John King, the only one left, was lucky. Hardly had the others died, when he was discovered by a group of Aborigines who lived in the outback themselves. 10. Three months later, a search party from Melbourne came and found him. Never would John King forget that day.

Chapter 19: Reported speech

1 It was out of this world!

1. the trip had been out of this world. He added that he had just come back from paradise. 2. he had been worried at first that he might not feel good in space. But he went on to say that he had felt great and that in fact he had never felt better in his entire life. 3. he hadn't adjusted to gravity yet. He explained that he was still used to weightlessness. 4. this had been a life-changing experience for Dennis. She added that she couldn't say if the Dennis Tito who returned to Earth would want the life he had had before, or the love he had had before. She believed that he might be quite a different person now. 5. Mr Tito had been great. He explained that he was not young, but that he was a very strong and very proud man. 6. Mr Tito's trip had been a misuse of the spacecraft. He explained that the space station was for research, not for tourism. 7. they were satisfied with this flight. They believed that Mr Tito's trip might be just the start of extraterrestrial tourism. 8. in future people wouldn't have to pay as much as he had. He explained / added / went on to say that when he got home, he was seriously thinking of starting a company that would specialize in space flights for tourists.

2 Sarah's nightmare in jail

Example of a summary:

Sarah said that she was glad to be home. She swore that she would do everything she could to make sure she would never have to go back to prison again. She said the whole experience had been a nightmare, and hoped she would never go back. She admitted that what she had done in November had been stupid. She described how she and her friends had lit a fire in a waste-bin and how it had got out of control and had done a lot of damage. She went on to say that the police had come, (of course,) and that in the end there had been a court case, and the judge had sentenced her. She remembered that she hadn't even packed a bag when she had gone to court and that she couldn't believe it when he gave her six months.

She explained that she had been in Styal, one of Britain's toughest jails for women and that she had been the youngest of 15 teenagers there. She said that it had been terrible there, but she thought that the prison officers had been really good. Sarah said that she had been released on bail after only six days and that the appeal might be heard in a couple of months. She remembered how glad she had been when she came out of the prison gate and her mum had been standing there. She went on to say that she was enjoying being at home. She felt she just wanted to relax with her family and friends.

3 What did he ask?

First he asked me if / whether I had ever had a job of any kind. Then he asked what I had liked about my Saturday job, and what I hadn't liked. He also wanted to know if / whether I enjoyed working with other people or if / whether could work best on my own.

Then he went on to ask if / whether I was keen on solving problems, how good my memory was and what my favourite subjects were. He wanted to know why I liked Maths so much. Then he asked me if / whether I would be interested in going to University, and finally he asked me if / whether I could imagine working in an office or a bank.

4 The Exe Estuary Code

1. Dog owners are asked to be considerate to other estuary users. They are told always to keep their pets under control and not to enter dog-free zones. 2. Walkers are advised not to put themselves or others at risk. They are warned to be aware of the dangers from rising tides, and from cliff edges. 3. Swimmers are told never to swim in the Navigation Channel. They are warned not to enter the water in areas marked by red flags and to follow instructions on signs. 4. Fishermen are asked to fish wisely and to avoid waste. They are told not to discard tackle and to return unwanted fish to the sea. 5. Birdwatchers are asked not to disturb wildlife. They are advised to enjoy watching the wildlife, but to keep their distance. 6. Windsurfers and other water users are told to keep to the appropriate area for their activity. They are warned not to enter bathing areas and asked to keep noise to a minimum.

5 On the telephone

1. Hello, this is David. Is Polly in? – Could you please give her a message? There's going to be a barbecue at Mark's tonight. Did Polly mention it to you? If Polly wants, I'll collect her at half past seven. I'll ring back later, unless she rings me. 2. Hello, this is Nicola. I've got Polly's Physics book. I took it by mistake during afternoon school and didn't discover it until I got home. I'll give it back to her on Monday. Do you think that will be all right? 3. Hello, this is Robin. Could you give Polly a message? I've been trying to get tickets for the show tomorrow, but the line has been busy all the time, so I haven't been able to book anything yet. There's no need for Polly to ring back.

6 That's odd!

Possible solutions:

1. you wanted to buy him a book / he didn't have a CD player / he didn't like listening to music. 2. you would be back by eight / you would come by bus. 3. they wanted to move to Richmond / they had bought a house / they had rented one / they couldn't afford to buy one. 4. the Brazilians spoke Portuguese / they spoke Portuguese there. 5. you couldn't stand her / you weren't going to see her again. 6. he wanted to study physics / to be an actor. 7. it was going to be warm and

sunny / it would be fine. 8. she had only invited a few friends / she was only going to have a small party.

7 Here and now – there and then

1. he would ring me up the next / following day / last Tuesday. 2. the bypass would be built the next / following year / two years ago. 3. living in London is very expensive. 4. he had only got back to work two days before / six days ago. 5. Dr Phillips would be away all the next / this week. 6. they arrived in Cyprus last Saturday.